THE SPIRITUAL WORLD
OF
THE
hobbit

Books by
James Stuart Bell

FROM BETHANY HOUSE PUBLISHERS

Angels, Miracles, and Heavenly Encounters

From the Library of A.W. Tozer

From the Library of Charles Spurgeon

Love Is a Flame

Love Is a Verb

Love Is a Verb (Devotional)

The Spiritual World of the Hobbit

THE SPIRITUAL WORLD
OF THE
hobbit

JAMES STUART BELL

WITH SAM O'NEAL

BETHANY HOUSE PUBLISHERS

a division of Baker Publishing Group
Minneapolis, Minnesota

© 2013 by Whitestone Communications, Inc.

James Stuart Bell with Sam O'Neal

Published by Bethany House Publishers
11400 Hampshire Avenue South
Bloomington, Minnesota 55438
www.bethanyhouse.com

Bethany House Publishers is a division of
Baker Publishing Group, Grand Rapids, Michigan

Printed in the United States of America

Library of Congress Cataloging-in-Publication Data
Bell, James S.
    The spiritual world of The Hobbit / James Stuart Bell with Sam O'Neal.
        p. cm.
    Includes bibliographical references.
    Summary: "This book is an exploration of the spiritual elements in Tolkien's classic, The Hobbit"—Provided by publisher.
    ISBN 978-0-7642-1020-4 (pbk. : alk. paper)
    1. Tolkien, J. R. R. (John Ronald Reuel), 1892-1973. Hobbit. 2. Christianity in literature. I. O'Neal, Sam, 1981- II. Title.
PR6039.O32H6334 2013
823'.912—dc23   2012028736

This book has not been authorized or endorsed by J. R. R. Tolkien's estate, *The Hobbit, The Lord of the Rings* trilogy, or anyone involved in *The Hobbit* or *The Lord of the Rings* movies.

Cover design by Kirk DouPonce, DogEared Design

13   14   15   16   17   18   19   7   6   5   4   3   2   1

To my grandchildren—
Wyatt James and Eden Belle,
Brogan William and Hudson Taylor,
and new baby Laird Seamus,
and our journeys together
—there and back again.

Contents

Contents

Acknowledgments

Much gratitude to Kyle Duncan, who encouraged me to pursue a book on Tolkien, as well as my talented editor Christopher Soderstrom. Many blessings upon Sam O'Neal for his timely assistance. And to my dear wife, Margaret, for her sustaining cups of tea.

Introduction

Perhaps you haven't yet read *The Hobbit*, even though people around you say it's a must-read—you just need a good reason to make this classic worth your while. Or maybe you've read every word of every volume related to Middle-earth and are seeking still another approach to deeper understanding and enjoyment.

Wherever you are along the way—at the very start, looking back and ready to travel all over again, or anywhere in between—I want to explore with you the spiritual dimension of this world, peopled with exotic creatures and fantastic adventures, yet consistent with the universe brought into being by our Creator and originating in the mind of an author with a firm belief in Christian revelation.

Elves. Goblins. Dwarves. Dragons . . . Creatures like these have populated the landscape of human mythology for thousands of years. Their adventures bridge generations and cultures, both capturing and kindling our imaginations. We love these tales because they grant us access to a world beyond our own.

Of course, with such a rich history of stories and storytellers, this world can feel rather dense at times. Characters and themes have a tendency to crowd together, sometimes overlapping or even contradicting one another. That's why it is such a rare and wonderful treat when something original and unexpected comes along and meaningfully contributes to the genre.

Something like a hobbit.

At first glance, hobbits don't seem to mesh well with their more mysterious or glamorous comrades—especially as heroes. They are small in stature. Their most notable attributes include a thick layer of fur on their feet, a thick layer of padding around their waists, and an ability to quickly, quietly disappear when "big folk" come lumbering near them.

And yet we must consider the words of the wizard Gandalf, spoken to Bilbo Baggins, when evaluating what hobbits are made of: "There is always more about you than anyone expects!"[1]

This is true of Bilbo, and it certainly is true of the tale that introduced him to our world.

First published in 1937, *The Hobbit* is one of the most popular books ever written. It has never been out of print, it has won numerous awards, and its success created a platform from which J. R. R. Tolkien could launch other works, including *The Lord of the Rings* and, posthumously, *The Silmarillion*.

Why This Book?

I am a Tolkien fan through and through. I've negotiated the terrain of Middle-earth a number of times; each journey there and back again has provided new discoveries, new joys. Consequently, this volume is both an outpouring of my appreciation for the world he fashioned and a record of my explorations there.

Still, you may wonder what else can be added to the conversation surrounding Tolkien's life and work. Do we really need another book about his books?

I think the answer is yes. The main reason is that, despite its immense success, several misconceptions remain concerning the adventures of Bilbo Baggins and company. Usually stemming from a lack of information, these misconceptions prevent readers from fully appreciating and benefitting from Tolkien's genius.

For example, many readers view *The Hobbit* as a simple, uncomplicated story, especially when compared to *The Lord of the Rings* trilogy. The tale is often perceived as a kind of appetizer—a snack before diving into the real "meat" of Middle-earth.

Such perceptions fall short of reality. While *The Hobbit* differs from Tolkien's larger works in style and tone, it is as superbly crafted and brilliantly polished as any of his creations. Indeed, because he took such pains to fine-tune the details of Bilbo's adventures, they are a vital piece that fits seamlessly into Tolkien's more expansive domain.

That's why I've packed so much information into this book. I believe that with a little help, anyone can appreciate the broader panorama of Middle-earth while venturing along with Bilbo, Gandalf, Thorin, and the rest.

Another common misconception is that *The Hobbit* is less spiritual than *The Lord of the Rings* and *The Silmarillion*. In fact many are unaware that spiritual themes permeate *all* of Tolkien's books.

Two basic facts will assist us here. First, J. R. R. Tolkien was a strong and outspoken Christian who spoke openly about his faith in all walks of life—from the halls of Oxford University to his dinner table at home and beyond. He even played a prominent role in C. S. Lewis's journey from atheist to Christ-follower.

Second, Tolkien formed Middle-earth on a foundation of Christian ideals and themes, which I will explore throughout this book. These motifs are straightforward in *The Silmarillion*, a broad history of Middle-earth from the world's creation all the way to Sauron's defeat. The spiritual elements in *The Lord of the Rings* are well documented and straightforwardly discerned.

In *The Hobbit*, Tolkien's theological underpinning is subtler and frequently beneath the surface. All the same, its current runs deep, and it touches every single aspect of the story.

This book is an effort to mine the spiritual signatures within that foundation, including Tolkien's emphasis on characters' moral development, the omnipresence of Providence, and the fiery battle between good and evil.

How to Read This Book

If you've ever experienced a guided tour of a complicated city or historical landmark, you know how valuable it is to have a professional tour guide.

Say you were going to spend a day in Jerusalem, for example. You could probably have a good time walking around and seeing the sites on your own. But imagine if you could spend the day with someone who really *knew* that city—someone who could explain the history, the mix of cultures, the best places for food, and so on. That experience would be much more compelling.

So here's how I encourage you to use this book. It's not a thirty-day devotional. It's not a summary of all *The Hobbit*'s minor plot elements. Rather, let it be your guide out of the Shire and into the wild lands of Middle-earth.

Toward that purpose, I've divided it into two parts.

Part 1 is meant to give a behind-the-scenes look at

Tolkien's authorial motivations. I examine why he crafted his mythology according to specific patterns and ideas and why he believed his writing was an act of worship and obedience. I also include a short history of Middle-earth, intended to foster a working knowledge of this ancient and ongoing story in which Bilbo Baggins plays a crucial role.

Part 2 will focus "between the pages" of *The Hobbit* itself. Each chapter corresponds with a chapter in Bilbo's journey—and I do recommend reading *The Hobbit* and this book together. My goal is to enhance your experience by providing a wealth of relevant insights and information.

For example, you'll learn the answers to the following questions:

- Who is Gandalf, and where did he come from?
- How did the different races of Middle-earth develop—(e.g., elves, dwarves, hobbits, men, and more)?
- What are the origins of evil creatures like goblins and trolls and dragons?
- How did Gollum find the Ring of Power?
- How does the afterlife work in Middle-earth?
- And much more.

Once again, and most important, each chapter will help you keep a finger on the spiritual pulse at the core of Tolkien's story—the theological themes that make *The Hobbit* a thoroughly Christian work of literature.

Grab a pocket-handkerchief, hop on a pony, and enjoy the ride!

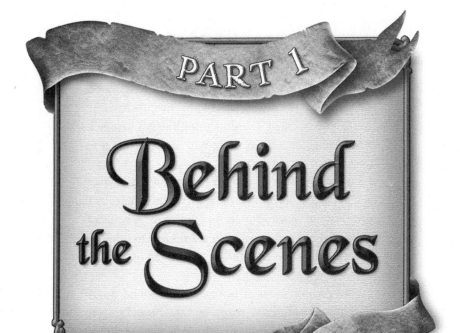

PART 1

Behind the Scenes

J. R. R. Tolkien is a towering figure of the twentieth century. Through the retrospective lens he'll remain known best as one of history's most popular storytellers—and rightfully so. The creativity, scope, and sheer adventure of his stories have captivated millions. Whether they're told through pages or pixels or anything else, they're certain to captivate millions more in the years to come.

But Tolkien was more than a storyteller. In his own day, he was revered as a man of many talents and interests. He was a soldier. A sportsman. A believer. A devoted husband and father. And for decades, he was a leading scholar and academician at Oxford University.

The combination of his experiences and qualities allowed Tolkien to transcend the boundaries of storytelling and become a profoundly accomplished *writer*—a master of words and worlds. His stories contain levels of poignancy, concreteness, and spiritual depth that entail some excavation and examination to fully appreciate.

So before we dive into *The Hobbit*, I want to go "Behind the Scenes" and explore the broader scope of Tolkien's goals and methods. I'll use these next three chapters to respond to three key questions:

1. What was Tolkien trying to accomplish? (What were his goals?)

2. How did he go about accomplishing those goals?

3. What was the result?

1

Faërie and Fairy Stories

Once upon a time.

The way you react to that phrase—the emotions it stirs up and how you feel thereafter—probably has a lot to do with the kinds of stories you've been exposed to. But whether those four words leave you feeling happy, wistful, bored, nostalgic, or even downright annoyed, it's undeniable that they help introduce some of the best-loved stories in the history of the world.

Fairy stories (or fairy tales) have been an important element of many cultures for many years. On one level, they have an academic appeal. They provide a common mythology and shared values. Most people will understand why it's a bad idea to "cry wolf," for example, because they've heard about *The Boy Who Cried Wolf.*

On a more practical level, people enjoy fairy stories simply because they are good stories. They provide fascinating characters who move through compelling plots. In other words, fairy stories are fun.

Both aspects appealed to J. R. R. Tolkien at different times in his life. Like many children, he was a fan during his younger years. He especially liked the many volumes of stories compiled by Andrew Lang, as well as various tales within Norse mythology.

During his maturation as a scholar, Tolkien took a much more academic (and passionate) interest in fairy stories. He studied their development over time—the way certain stories morphed and changed when moving from culture to culture. He delved into the historical roots of characters. He even explored the impact of fairy stories on the development of different words and languages, and vice versa.

Not surprisingly, Tolkien's passion for these stories influenced his own fictional world. In fact, one of the most central facts about *The Hobbit* is that Tolkien intended it to be a fairy story in the very best sense of the term.

Lucky for us, he succeeded.

Definitions

Fairy story can mean different things to different people. Some view fairy stories as silly narratives written primarily for children. Others define them as tales whose main characters are fairies, pixies, brownies, elves, and other magical creatures. Still others think of them as adventures that are touched by some element of magic or the supernatural.

We know exactly what Tolkien thought about fairy stories because he was not shy about offering his opinions on this subject. And those opinions lend a great deal of insight into his views on *The Hobbit* and other stories within his mythology.

In 1939, two years after *The Hobbit* was published, Tolkien gave a presentation called "On Fairy-Stories" as part of the Andrew Lang Lecture Series at the University of St. Andrews, Scotland. In 1947—while writing *The Lord of the Rings* trilogy—Tolkien revised this presentation for publication in a book called *Essays Presented to Charles Williams.*

"On Fairy-Stories" was Tolkien's attempt at both explaining and exploring fairy stories as a valid genre of literature. What makes the essay fascinating for our purposes is that Tolkien was working through it at the same time he was creating what would become arguably the best fairy stories of the twentieth century: *The Hobbit* and *The Lord of the Rings.*

So, what *is* a fairy story?

To be fair, Tolkien wasn't entirely certain. Or to say it another way, he felt that the borders separating fairy stories from other literary genres were hard to define. He admitted this within the first few paragraphs of his essay:

> In that realm a man may, perhaps, find himself fortunate to have wandered, but its very richness and strangeness tie the tongue of a traveler who would report them. And while he is there it is dangerous for him to ask too many questions, lest the gates should be shut and the keys be lost.[1]

Still, Tolkien did highlight a number of characteristics that must be present in order for a story to be considered a true "fairy story." I'll take a moment to briefly explain each of these characteristics, and then we'll see how they impact *The Hobbit* in particular.

A Touch of Mystery

First, Tolkien believed fairy stories should contain an element of the mysterious, even mystical—something beyond what we'd call the "real world."

> A fairy-story is one which touches on or uses Faërie, whatever its own main purpose may be: satire, adventure, morality, fantasy. Faërie itself may perhaps most nearly be translated by Magic—but it is a magic of a peculiar mood and power, at the furthest pole from the vulgar devices of the laborious, scientific, magician.[2]

If you don't recognize that word *Faërie*, don't worry. It's not common today, nor was it used frequently in 1939. For Tolkien, the term encompassed a magical and mysterious reality outside the ordinary routines and practices of everyday life. In many ways, Tolkien viewed Faërie as an ideal reality—what our world should have been like if it weren't messed up by the chaos and noise and confusion of sin.

Yet this reality, what Tolkien sometimes referred to as the Perilous Realm, was not completely separated from "normal life" routines and practices. It could be reached and touched by ordinary people. (Or, perhaps more accurately, it could reach out and touch them.)

For Tolkien, then, a fairy story succeeded when an author succeeded in accessing this realm during the process of creating a story—and, by extension, granting a similar sort of access to those who experience the author's creation.

A Touch of Fantasy

The second characteristic of fairy stories is similar to the first, although the two have a cause/effect relationship. In order to help readers experience the mysterious realm of Faërie, Tolkien believed fairy stories should include elements that are fantastical—people and places and situations that break through the boundaries of normal, everyday life.

This is where imagination comes in: The author needs the ability to conceive of what Tolkien referred to as "arresting strangeness." Yet being able to imagine these elements is not enough. The author must also possess the artistic skill needed to incorporate those elements into a working story.

In other words, it's not terribly difficult to imagine a creature like a hobbit—take a man, make him smaller and shoeless, and you've got a good start. But it's quite another matter to place that creature into a story in such a way that we care about him and worry about what happens to him.

As you would imagine, *The Hobbit* is a wonderful example of the use of fantasy. There are countless stories of humble protagonists who become heroic after passing through the crucible of trials and tribulations. What makes Bilbo's story a work of fantasy is that it includes goblins and dragons and magic rings that turn people invisible—and hobbits too, of course.

A Touch of Truth

Finally, Tolkien believed a fairy story must be presented as true in order for its magic to have any effect on the reader. And he wrote about this in very definitive terms:

> It is at any rate essential to a genuine fairy-story, as distinct from the employment of this form for less or debased purposes, that it should be presented as "true. . . ." Since the fairy story deals with "marvels," it cannot tolerate any frame or machinery suggesting that the whole story in which they occur is a figment or illusion.[3]

For Tolkien, then, any story that turned out to be a dream or other form of hallucination could not be considered a fairy story. (He specifically disqualified Lewis Carroll's *Alice* stories for this reason; I wonder what he thought about *The Wizard of Oz*?) The same is true for stories that overuse technology in order to manufacture otherworldly situations.

He believed that such artificial explanations for a story's fantastical elements essentially were tantamount to pulling out the rug from underneath a reader's feet—they *break the magic*. This has a lot to do with Tolkien's idea of "subcreation," the subject of this book's chapter 2.

Of Faërie and Mr. Baggins

Perhaps you're wondering why all this is important for a proper understanding of *The Hobbit* today. And given the title of this book, you may be thinking that these theories have little to do with finding the spiritual themes tucked inside Bilbo's adventure.

Both questions have a straightforward answer: In order to suitably explore *The Hobbit*, we must grasp what Tolkien was trying to accomplish when he wrote it. We need to get our minds around what he was trying to do. And what he was trying to do was write a fairy story.

Knowing his parameters and definitions gives us a peek at the bones of Bilbo's quest. It's like seeing the structure and foundation of a house before the walls are painted and the shingles tacked into place.

But Tolkien wasn't satisfied with writing just any old fairy story. He was a connoisseur of the genre and a respected literary critic; he wanted to represent fairy stories in the best possible light. He wanted Bilbo's journey to represent the very best of what a fairy story could achieve—an escapade that allowed him to experience the magic of Faërie as he wrote, and a story that offered the same opportunity to his readers.

Fortunately, he identified the perfect vehicle to accomplish this enchantment: Bilbo Baggins.

It's been well documented that Tolkien characterized Bilbo so as to reflect many of his own values. For example, here is an excerpt from a letter to a reader:

> I am in fact a hobbit in all but size. I like gardens, trees, and unmechanized farmlands; I smoke a pipe, and like good plain food (unrefrigerated), but detest French cooking; I like, and even dare to wear in these dull days, ornamental waistcoats. I am fond of mushrooms (out of a field); have a very simple sense of humour (which even my appreciative critics find tiresome); I go to bed late and get up late (when possible). I do not travel much.[4]

But it's also true that the hobbit represents the values of many who read Tolkien's work—people like you and me. At the beginning of the story, Bilbo places a high value on safety and comfort. He is a good enough fellow but very much a consumer and very focused on himself. In other words, he is a typical Western person at his core.

Given those realities, when safe, comfortable Bilbo meets the wizard Gandalf on the third page of *The Hobbit*, we know he is about to be confronted with the power of Faërie. We also know that the rest of his adventures in that Perilous Realm will provide opportunities for growth and change in the midst of danger and potential loss. In fact, the only thing that can be said for certain is that Bilbo will not come out the same.

And if we allow ourselves to become enchanted by the tale, neither will we.

2

Tolkien as Sub-Creator

Imagine the following scene: You're strolling through a park when you come across two young men sitting on a bench. Spread around them, on the bench and on the ground at their feet, are many, many comic books.

The books are open; a breeze is ruffling the pages. You notice the comics are of the superhero variety. You get several glimpses of a muscular man in a blue outfit—there's a large *S* on his chest, and he appears to be wearing red underpants. You also see several drawings of a more slender man in a red jumpsuit. Is that a yellow lightning bolt zigzagging across his chest?

As you pass the bench, you catch a few snippets of conversation:

First man: "If you think The Flash is faster than Superman, you're crazy. Superman can fly!"

Second man: "So what? Birds can fly—are you saying birds would be faster than The Flash?"

First man: "No. I'm saying The Flash has to put his feet on the ground to run. He builds up a lot of resistance that way. Superman just zooms through the air—he's more aerodynamical."

Second man: "That's not even a word. Besides, if it's true that The Flash can violate the laws of physics, then I think . . ."

Maybe you've witnessed a debate like that. Maybe you've even participated. We're a culture that loves stories, after all—movies, TV, books, video games, and more. We love extraordinary characters who perform extraordinary feats in extraordinary situations.

And because these characters usually inhabit different worlds, many of which are built with different rules than those of our own, it's natural for us to compare. *Could* The Flash be faster than Superman? Who's more romantic, Mr. Darcy or Jack Dawson? Who'd win if James Bond fought the A-Team?

When we engage in such comparisons, we're validating one of J. R. R. Tolkien's core beliefs about storytelling: the practice of "sub-creation."

Primary and Secondary

Once more, Tolkien maintained that the main goal of a fairy story is to help its author and reader experience something magical and, potentially, transformational—an outside reality he identified as Faërie or the Perilous Realm. In order for us to be moved toward reaching that realm, fairy stories should include elements of fantasy—people and places and situations marked by an "arresting strangeness." At the same time, those people and places and situations cannot be presented in a cheesy or unbelievable way; they must be introduced and developed as if they were genuine and real.

Right away, that should spark some questions for anyone who dreams of one day writing like Tolkien. In fact, it should spark some questions for anyone who wants to understand the man's own writing.

For one: How does an author go about writing a story that's both fantastical *and* rational? How is it possible to craft something containing the mystery of Faërie and also the ring of veracity?

The answer, according to Tolkien, is to operate as a sub-creator in order to build a Secondary World.

PRIMARY WORLD

Take a minute to look at your environment—everything that's around you, wherever you might be. If you're indoors, look at the walls on either side; thump your feet down on the floorboards or tiles. If you're outdoors, try to find the sun and feel its light; listen for a breeze rustling over grass.

In Tolkien's terms, the elements and forces you just observed represent the Primary World. It's the world currently motoring through the twenty-first century. It's the world of stock markets and savings accounts; Republicans and Democrats; gravity and thermodynamics.

Don't let yourself label it as the "real" world, though. Tolkien certainly would not have done so. It may be the *physical* world, yes, but that doesn't necessarily make it more "real" than other dimensions.

The most important thing to know about the Primary World isn't who lives there or what may be found within it; rather, it's Who made it.

The Primary World is the reality that was built (and is still maintained) by God, the Creator.

SECONDARY WORLD

Obviously, human beings lack the capacity to form their own Primary Worlds. We are created beings, and so we cannot serve as creators.

But we *can* function as sub-creators.

Tolkien held that by combining imagination and art, we are able to build Secondary Worlds in which the elements of our fairy stories can operate. When they succeed, these Secondary Worlds both reflect and transcend what we sense and perceive within the Primary World—they should have a similar foundation yet also contain elements of fantasy (the "fantastic").

While it's true that a Secondary World exists only as thought and creative energy, it would be a mistake to label it as "fake" and the Primary World as "real." For Tolkien's part, I don't think even he would have been comfortable talking about the Primary World as "physical" (or "tangible") and our Secondary Worlds as simply "mental" or "imaginative."

Rather, again, what separates the two types of worlds is who does the building. The Primary World, built from nothing by the Creator, is an example of creation. Secondary Worlds, crafted by sub-creators from what the Creator has given us, are examples of sub-creation.

Believe it or not, Tolkien felt that adding fantasy to a Secondary World—incorporating those elements of "arresting strangeness"—is the easy part. He viewed it in terms of "playing" with what already exists in the Primary World, as a child manipulates Play-Doh to fashion different forms.

For example, we might see a horse and think, *What would happen if such an animal had wings and could*

Tolkien as Sub-Creator

fly? Or we might consider an "already existing" fantastical notion, such as a magic wand, and ask, *What if there
was a network of schools that taught children the ins and
outs of magic?*

In Tolkien's view, the truly difficult task is creating a
Secondary World that rings true enough for fairy stories
to operate successfully. Thinking of a training ground for
wizards is one thing; it's quite another to come up with
locations, students, teachers, magical laws, villains, heroes,
and all the rest.

Remember that a fairy story must be presented as actual
in order for the elements of fantasy to be accepted by the
reader and without breaking the story's magic. For that
reason, the Secondary World through which that story is
told needs to have a realistic feel—it needs to make sense,
otherwise the magic dissolves.

Here's how Tolkien explained this concept:

> Anyone inheriting the fantastic device of human language
> can say *the green sun*. Many can then imagine or picture
> it. But that is not enough. . . .
>
> To make a Secondary World inside which the green sun
> will be credible, commanding Secondary Belief, will prob-
> ably require labour and thought, and will certainly demand
> a special skill, a kind of elvish craft. Few attempt such dif-
> ficult tasks. But when they are attempted and in any degree
> accomplished then we have a rare achievement of Art.[1]

That term *Secondary Belief* is important as well. It
refers to what happens when readers get pulled into a
story—when they become immersed with the characters
and landscape to where they think and act as if the story
were real.

Remember the two guys arguing about the relative
"speeds" of Superman and The Flash? That illustrates

31

Secondary Belief brought about by an effectively crafted Secondary World.

Of course, people who read about superheroes know they're not "real"—they're not a part of the Primary World, anyway. We recognize that human beings can't actually vault towers or run a hundred miles per hour, just as we're aware that dragons and hobbits don't exist in "real" life.

Yet when an author convinces us—wittingly or unwittingly—to forget what we know and instead accept what he or she is telling us to be true, then we have embraced the reality of that Secondary World. We have opened ourselves to the possibility of fantasy, of "arresting strangeness," which means we also have opened ourselves to the transformative potential of Faërie and the Perilous Realm.

That is the power of sub-creation.

ℜeflections

As you consider J. R. R. Tolkien's views on storytelling and sub-creation, it's important to know he wasn't a fan of allegories, and he never set out to make allegorical connections within his stories.

An allegory is "a poem, play, picture, etc., in which the apparent meaning of the characters and events is used to symbolize a deeper moral or spiritual meaning."[2] In other words, a story that uses allegory is primarily driven by symbols that point away from the story in order to connect it with a more abstract or conceptual design.

C. S. Lewis's *The Lion, the Witch, and the Wardrobe* is an excellent example. Aslan was an intentional symbol of Jesus, for instance, and his death on the Stone Table (which itself represents the stone tablets of the law Moses brought down from Sinai) is directly connected to Christ's death on the cross.

Tolkien preferred to avoid such explicit associations because he felt they limited the realism of a story's Secondary World. By conspicuously pointing away from the story, he felt that allegorics broke the enchantment he sought to create through it.

Therefore, as I explore the spiritual themes within *The Hobbit*, I will not claim that a moment in Bilbo's experience "symbolizes" an aspect of the Christian life. I will not argue that a wise word from Gandalf represents a scriptural doctrine. I will not try to demonstrate direct links between Tolkien's imagery and specific ideas or people in the Bible.

Instead, I'll point out the ways that Tolkien's Secondary World—in this case, the story of Bilbo's adventure—reflects the values and truths God built into the Primary World. I'll highlight the biblical and spiritual foundations Tolkien emulated and adapted during the process of writing his stories.

Sub-Creation as Worship

If you've followed me this far, you probably agree that sub-creation seems like a pretty good way to tell a story—when it's done suitably. And the success of Tolkien's works would certainly lend credence to that thought.

But for Tolkien, performing as a sub-creator was about more than good writing. It was about good worship too.

God is our Creator, and yet He is more than that—He is *creative*. The divine Craftsman shaped our Primary World with more than merely functional appeal. God is the source of all beauty and loveliness; He is the cause of riotous colors and diverse textures and inspiring forms.

The Scriptures point to these creative qualities in several places, and these attributes are referred to or implied in several more. Here are a few examples:

The Lord said to Moses, "See, I have chosen Bezalel son of Uri, the son of Hur, of the tribe of Judah, and I have filled him with the Spirit of God, with wisdom, with understanding, with knowledge and with all kinds of skills—to make artistic designs for work in gold, silver and bronze, to cut and set stones, to work in wood, and to engage in all kinds of crafts."

Exodus 31:1–5

The Lord spoke to Job out of the storm. He said:

"Who is this that obscures my plans
with words without knowledge?
Brace yourself like a man;
I will question you,
and you shall answer me.

Where were you when I laid the earth's foundation?
Tell me, if you understand.
Who marked off its dimensions? Surely you know!
Who stretched a measuring line across it?
On what were its footings set,
or who laid its cornerstone—
while the morning stars sang together
and all the angels shouted for joy?"

Job 38:1–7

You, Lord, are our Father.
We are the clay, you are the potter;
we are all the work of your hand.

Isaiah 64:8

This is the God whom Tolkien, a devout Christian, worshiped. He certainly appreciated our world's magnificent craftsmanship, and we can assume he expressed that appreciation through prayer and song.

But for Tolkien, his truest moments of worship came when he went beyond admiration and endeavored upon something more concrete: imitation. He knew that not only do human beings serve a creative God, we also are created in the very image of that creative God:

> In the beginning God created the heavens and the earth. . . .
> Then God said, "Let us make mankind in our image, in our likeness, so that they may rule over the fish in the sea and the birds in the sky, over the livestock and all the wild animals, and over all the creatures that move along the ground."
>
> So God created mankind in his own image,
> in the image of God he created them;
> male and female he created them.
>
> Genesis 1:1, 26–27

When we engage in creativity, we do more than embellish or exaggerate what God has created in this world. To engage in creativity is to imitate our creative Father. In so doing we emulate one of His key characteristics and thus offer a vital form of worship.

Tolkien explored this concept in his essay "On Fairy-Stories," although he approached the topic in two distinct ways.

First, he mentioned a letter he received from a reader who believed his sub-creative journeys into fantasy and mythology were nothing more than "lies." Fittingly, Tolkien responded (and in doing so defended the high art of fantasy) by writing a poem. Later in the essay, Tolkien used more conventional prose to explain:

> Fantasy remains a human right: we make in our measure and in our derivative mode, because we are made: and not only made, but made in the image and likeness of a Maker.[3]

Intriguingly, these descriptions may not have been his most convincing method of clarifying the complicated connection between sub-creation and worship. In my opinion, this distinction belongs to a fascinating dialogue between two characters in one of his sub-creations: *The Silmarillion.*

Near the beginning of that book, Aulë, an angel-like being, attempts to create a race of beings he can love and teach within the confines of Middle-earth. He was meant to wait for the coming of the elves into the world, but in his joy and overzealousness, Aulë instead created the dwarves as a race apart.

When confronted by the divine Creator, Aulë is humble and repentant. While he understands he was wrong, his explanation for his deeds plainly and deeply connects with Tolkien's ideas about sub-creation. He says that although he was impatient and has "fallen into folly," he was created to make things. In this he was imitating his father, the Creator, rather than mocking him. That's sub-creation. And that's a powerful form of worship.

3

A Short History of Middle-Earth

If you're familiar with *The Lord of the Rings* trilogy, you may recall the events described therein taking place during Middle-earth's "third age." Did you know that there's an extant history of its first and second ages as well? Or that Middle-earth is not the only realm in Tolkien's larger mythology?

I've already alluded to the extended history of Tolkien's world—what is often referred to as his mythology or legendarium, a literary collection of legends. Most of it is recorded in *The Silmarillion*, which functions as a kind of Old Testament in connection with *The Hobbit* and *The Lord of the Rings*. Other information can also be gleaned from the four-part *Unfinished Tales* and the twelve-volume

The History of Middle-Earth, compiled and edited by Christopher Tolkien, based on his father's notes.

Note: The pages immediately following will not often refer to *Hobbit* characters like Gandalf or Bilbo or Thorin. I've found it extremely helpful to have a working knowledge of this background history when reading *The Hobbit*. The details and intricacies of Bilbo's journey take on more significance when we realize the larger drama into which he is pulled.

In the Beginning

There are several ways in which *The Silmarillion*'s wonderfully written beginning chapters parallel the first chapters of the book of Genesis.

Here is the opening paragraph:

> There was Eru, the One, who in Arda is called Ilúvatar; and he made first the Ainur, the Holy Ones, that were the offspring of his thought, and they were with him before aught else was made. And he spoke to them, propounding to them themes of music; and they sang before him, and he was glad. . . .[1]

Within Tolkien's universe, *Ilúvatar* is the divine Creator whose power and acts are reflections of how the Bible describes God. The *Ainur*, Ilúvatar's first creations, are similar in function to angels.

The "themes of music" ultimately became the world's creation—Ilúvatar transformed the details of the song into material reality. He also granted the Ainur a vision of what would happen in the world, including the eventual creation of elves and men.

After this revelation, Ilúvatar offered the Ainur the opportunity to enter the world as lords and stewards. Those that accepted would be tied to it; immortal, they could not leave, could not rejoin Ilúvatar, until its end. These also would be charged with everything from carving out physical structures and geographical features to teaching elves and men about truth and holiness.

Several Ainur accepted this invitation and entered the world. The more powerful would be called the Valar. The lesser beings were called the Maiar.

Fallen Angel

The character and behavior of Melkor, the most powerful of the Ainur, reflects Satan's, for from the beginning, rather than submit to the will of Ilúvatar, Melkor desired to create out of and according to his own volition. His thoughts disrupted the Great Music and engendered discord and chaos among the Ainur. Worse, many of the Ainur around Melkor "began to attune their music to his."[2]

Interestingly, Ilúvatar did not forbid Melkor from making his own music, nor did he prevent the dissonance it caused. Instead, Ilúvatar wove another musical theme, one that flowed around Melkor's music and stole its power. The result is a wonderful depiction of the conflict between good and evil throughout Tolkien's world (and ours).

In many ways, this is the essence of that clash in Tolkien's legendarium, including *The Hobbit*.

Among the Ainur sent into the world, Melkor brought discord and strife. He and the ones that followed him are the chief instigators of evil and violence and pain throughout that realm's history. (Melkor was also called Morgoth, the Black Foe of the World.) However, the forces of good were not idle; the will of Ilúvatar *would* be carried out, and they fought back, sometimes through bold action yet often defeating the forces of evil in subtle and surprising ways (the means of which included a few hobbits).

Darkness and Light

In Tolkien's writing, this conflict is often represented through the imagery of light and darkness. That was the case at the beginning.

When the Valar first came as physical beings, they formed two great lamps to provide light for the world. Both were set on tall pillars—one at the northern pole, and the other at the south. But Melkor and his forces knocked down the pillars, wreaking havoc across Middle-earth. In the resulting pandemonium, the realm's geography was scarred and broken.

The Valar then left Middle-earth and set up residence in Aman, across the sea at the world's western edge. They made their capital at Valinor and fortified this land against Melkor, making it a "blessed realm"[3]—a Middle-earthly paradise.

To replace the destroyed lamps, the Valar created the Two Trees of Valinor. The flowers of Telperion, the elder tree, emitted silver dew that shone across Aman. The flowers of Laurelin, the younger tree, shone with a golden flame. Both trees waxed and waned on alternating cycles every twelve hours; this is how the concept of time first came into the world. With the genesis of these trees, the Valar began keeping track of hours and days.

The trees' light did not extend across the sea to Middle-earth, where Melkor and his followers were fortifying their own fortresses: Utumno in the north and Angband by the northwestern shores of the Great Sea. But the Valar set new constellations of stars in the sky to burn in the darkness as a challenge to Melkor and a reminder of the will of Ilúvatar.

The Elves

It was under the light of these constellations that the elves first awoke in Middle-earth, and ever since, they have loved twilight more than any other time of day. (In chapter 3 of *The Hobbit,* Bilbo mentions elvish singing as something not to be missed in June under the stars.)

When, eventually, the Valar became aware of the elves, they invited them to live in the land of Aman. Many of the elves accepted and made the long journey west to Valinor. Many others chose to remain in Middle-earth and live under the stars—the wood elves of Mirkwood, for example, were among those that stayed behind and never saw the light of Valinor.

Before the elves made their journey, the Valar attacked and broke the gates of Utumno in a terrible battle. In the end, Melkor was captured, carried back across the sea in chains, declared guilty of his crimes, and sentenced to remain locked away for three full ages.

During that period, the elves that relocated to Aman thrived. They grew in wisdom and skill through learning from the Valar. And as the elves are immortal beings, they grew in number as well.

The greatest of these was Fëanor, whose name means "spirit of fire." Powerful in mind and body, he also was skilled in metalwork and the art of making gems. Fëanor crafted the Silmarils—three jewels containing mingled light from the Two Trees of Valinor. These, his greatest creation, likewise were the undoing of his own family and many of the elves.

At the end of three ages, Melkor was brought back before the Valar. Because he confessed his crimes and promised to repent of his sin, he was set free and allowed to live in Valinor. Yet he deceived the Valar. While in Valinor, he convinced many elves that they were living as slaves in Aman when they should have been roaming free in the lands of Middle-earth.

Once his lies had taken hold, Melkor escaped the Valar—only to return with Ungoliant, a dreadful spider. Together they destroyed the Two Trees of Valinor, killing their light. Melkor also stole the Silmarils before fleeing back to Middle-earth and again taking up residence in the halls of Angband.

When the Valar examined the trees, they were able to produce one last fruit from each. These hallowed treasures were then set in the sky as the Sun and the Moon.

Rebellion and War

After Melkor's attack, a segment of elves called the Noldor rebelled against the Valar, determined to return to Middle-earth and build their own kingdoms. They also wanted to take vengeance on Melkor and reclaim the Silmarils—Fëanor (along with his sons) swore a terrible oath to kill any living thing that stood between him and the jewels. The Noldor killed other elves during this rebellion and so were banished from returning to Valinor.

The Noldor spread throughout Middle-earth and did establish several kingdoms and strongholds, most notably Nargothrond and Gondolin. However, the elves were also hampered by division, strife, and mistrust—especially because of the sons of Fëanor and their oath.

Over the span of centuries, the elves made alliances and waged war against Melkor and his forces. They won several victories and were able to generate many decades of peace and prosperity. In the end, however, Melkor wore them down through treachery and by preying on their lack of trust. One by one the mighty kingdoms of the elves were broken.

Things looked darkest for the elves (and for Middle-earth) after the destruction of Gondolin, which had been the fairest and most powerful of the elvish strongholds. But then something unexpected happened.

Eärendil was a prince of Gondolin, the son of a human father and an elvish mother. He escaped the devastation, and, years later, built a mighty ship to sail across the western seas. He hoped to find the Valar and plead for help against Melkor. Because he carried the only Silmaril that had been recovered from Melkor, Eärendil succeeded in his quest.

The Valar heard his petition and decided to act. They crossed the sea once more and laid siege to Angband. Ultimately they recaptured Melkor and dragged him back to Valinor. Again put on trial and again found guilty, this time Melkor was banished from the world and sent out into the Void.

These events marked the end of the first age of Middle-earth.

The Coming of Men

Human beings awoke during this first age, and several groups made alliances with the elves. (Others, with Melkor.) Tuor, father of Eärendil, was a mighty warrior for the forces of good.

But *The Silmarillion*'s main human story is with the people of Númenor.

After the final battle between the Valar and Melkor, the men who had joined sides with the elves were given a land of their own—a great island between Middle-earth and the shores of Aman, which they named Númenor. They built immense ships and sailed the oceans to different points within Middle-earth and beyond. Even so, because they were mortal, they were forbidden from sailing westward to Aman where the Valar lived.

The Númenórians grew in knowledge and power for hundreds of years and became a great kingdom.

Unfortunately, Melkor's overthrow did not destroy the forces of evil in Middle-earth. Sauron, who had been Melkor's greatest lieutenant, escaped the Valar when Melkor was defeated. After the Valar returned to the west, Sauron set himself up as a second Dark Lord in Middle-earth, continuing to fight against elves and men.

Eventually the Númenórians grew strong enough to overthrow Sauron. He surrendered, was taken to Númenor as a captive, promised to repent of his evil, and even became a counselor to the king. And as Melkor had done in Valinor, he deceived those whose destruction he secretly desired.

Gradually, Sauron would convince the people of Númenor that humans should not have to suffer death—they should be immortal like the elves and the Valar. He persuaded the king that they could attain immortality; the Númenórians took his advice to rebel against the Valar, to sail west to Aman.

They were destroyed. Ilúvatar himself punished them by breaking the foundations of his creation: The world, which had been flat, was made round, and no longer could people sail to the Blessed Realm of Aman. Only elves, who knew the secret path, would be welcome to voyage into the west when they grew weary of Middle-earth. (At the end of *The Lord of the Rings*, Bilbo and Frodo accompany the final group of elves to make this voyage.)

During this divine remaking, the entire island of Númenor was cast into the sea. (Herein, Tolkien was retelling the story of Atlantis.)

Fortunately for human beings, nine ships of Nú-menórian royalty who were still faithful to Ilúvatar sailed away from the island before it sank. They were carried to Middle-earth, where they established the kingdoms of Arnor in the north and Gondor in the south. Their leader was Elendil; his sons were Isildur and Anárion.

Though Sauron had been caught in the destruction of Númenor, his spirit was not destroyed. He would return to Middle-earth and again take his place as a Dark Lord. But while his power increased, so did the strength of the alliance between the Númenórian remnant and the elves still there.

The forces of good and evil eventually clashed in another battle—the last "moment" in the *second* age of Middle-earth. Sauron was overthrown when Isildur sliced the One Ring from his finger with the shards of Narsil. Yet Isildur was killed on his way home from the battle, and the ring was lost.

Peace held sway in Middle-earth for many years before Sauron, once more, began to rise in might. Though Middle-earth's third age largely would be a time of harmony, it concludes with the events contained in *The Hobbit* and *The Lord of the Rings*.

PART 2

Between the Pages

Bilbo Baggins, a hobbit, plain and small, is alone and far from home. He stands in a tunnel cut through the roots of an ancient mountain. Behind him are the stars, a cool night breeze, and his friends. Ahead of him are foul vapors and an ominous red glow—sure signs that Smaug, the dragon, huge and horrifying, awaits.

Bilbo doesn't know it, but he has reached the crux of his journey. Not the journey from Bag End to the Lonely Mountain and back again. That quest encompasses the fates of dwarves, goblins, wizards, men, and more. Indeed, the mission to defeat Smaug and restore the King under the Mountain is a small chapter in a much larger tale—one that stretches from the creation of the world to the actions of another hobbit, Bilbo's nephew, inside Mount Doom.

No, what Bilbo has reached is his own pivotal moment. He must make a decision in the middle of that tunnel. Will he give in to fear and turn back? Or will he press forward and take his place among the heroes of Middle-earth?

If you've read *The Hobbit*, or even if you've read *The Lord of the Rings*, you know which path Bilbo ultimately chooses. But you may not know why he does so—or why that particular choice is so important.

By the time you finish this book, you'll know this and much, much more.

1

A Comfortable Life

It's no surprise that an author would provide the best description of his or her own book. Here is a snippet from J. R. R. Tolkien's introduction to the original edition of *The Hobbit*, published in 1937:

> If you care for journeys there and back, out of the comfortable Western world, over the edge of the Wild, and home again, and can take an interest in a humble hero (blessed with a little wisdom and a little courage and considerable good luck), here is a record of such a journey and such a traveler.[1]

If we care, indeed! Many millions of us have read about the adventures of Bilbo Baggins from Hobbiton, the Shire—and we have cared. We have laughed with him, grieved with him, fearfully shivered with him, and triumphantly celebrated with him. Such is the power of his story.

And yet, if we're honest, we have to admit that our first glimpse of the estimable Mr. Baggins reveals a great deal of *humble* and very little *hero*.

Bilbo Baggins B.A.

Don't all good stories begin with a problem to be solved? Right away in chapter 1 of *The Hobbit*, Tolkien makes it clear that the problem in this tale lies with the titular character: the hobbit Bilbo Baggins.

At first glance, we might think the problem occurs when the respectable Bilbo is hoodwinked into joining a dangerous venture. But we'd be wrong. Or we might think it has to do with his stature: short and pudgy with "little or no magic"[2] is not a strong combination for a protagonist. That's closer to the mark, but still wrong.

Rather, the main problem Tolkien wants us to see at the beginning of this book lies *inside* the hobbit. Bilbo Baggins B.A. (Before Adventure) possesses a major character flaw. His highest priorities are comfort and safety, and he displays several vices when those concerns are disturbed or threatened.

For example, when Gandalf first speaks with Bilbo, he mentions that he is looking for someone to share in an adventure. The hobbit is rude in response. He reads his morning letters and pretends nobody else is there, hoping the old man will just go away.

Later, when Gandalf's intervention compels Bilbo to host an unexpected party for thirteen hungry dwarves, again and again the hobbit demonstrates a glutton's over-concern with (and over-fondness for) food.

Worst of all, Bilbo Baggins B.A. lacks the virtues of bravery and courage. In other words, he's a coward. And while this is a cardinal sin in any generation, it's noted as particularly so in one that has endured one terrible war and teeters on the brink of another.

What's the Problem?

From a distance, Bilbo's shortcomings and faults may not seem crucial or perhaps even significant. After all, deep down, lots of people are cowardly. Many of us behave boorishly at times. And who doesn't ever succumb to over-indulgence? What's the big deal?

There are at least two reasons these sentiments don't apply to this hobbit.

A Heroic Hobbit

The first reason for highlighting these flaws is that Bilbo was created to be so much more than a cravenly self-centered, safety-obsessed coward. In fact, Bilbo Baggins was designed to be a hero.

Tolkien clearly points us in this direction during the events of the unexpected party in chapter 1. Initially, the hobbit's attitude and reactions are normal enough. He's confused, frustrated, and annoyed as a throng of uninvited guests are taking advantage of him. We sympathize with his predicament.

But when the dwarves begin to sing about the deeds and treasures of their ancient ancestors, we see a different side of Bilbo. He wants to see mountains, and trees, and waterfalls and "wear a sword instead of a walking stick"[3]

In this key moment, larger forces are at work around Bilbo. He begins catching hold of visions and notions bigger than and beyond himself—themes outside his cozy and isolated existence. A small, struggling seed of courage does exist in the hobbit's heart, awaiting opportunity to sprout and grow.

Furthermore, Tolkien wants us to see that these desires have always been inside Bilbo. They were not planted by the dwarves' song; rather, they were stirred and roused. There is a dozing, undernourished conqueror inside this pudgy little frame—one he doesn't even recognize.

However, this flash of awakening doesn't last long. The wood-fire Bilbo "sees" in the distance reminds him of dragons, which reminds him of danger. And in the face of even imagined peril, he wilts. He would have fled down to cringe behind the beer barrels in his cellar if Gandalf and the dwarves hadn't stopped him.

To make sure we don't overlook the import of Bilbo's constitutional weakness, Tolkien records an even more cowardly (and hilarious) episode soon thereafter. When Thorin implies that members of the company might be killed during the expedition, something snaps inside the hobbit. He shrieks and kneels on the floor, shaking like a bowl of jelly. Then he falls on his back, repeatedly calls out gibberish, and refuses to say anything else for a long time.

It's a wretched, pathetic display for a would-be champion.

A Coming Conflict

There's another reason for emphasizing the fat in Bilbo's moral fiber: He's about to be drafted into a conflict that's been raging for thousands of years. He will not stay detached from the ultimate struggle between good and evil.

This war has been spurred on by the valiant deeds and sacrifices of elves and men, Valar and Maiar, since the world's creation. Now, at this time things are rushing toward a climax. The Shadow is rapidly amassing advantage and gaining strength; the forces of good are scattered and thin. In order for good finally to triumph, something unexpected must happen.

As it happens, Bilbo has much to do with this something unexpected—although not even Gandalf fully understands this when he selects Bilbo to be the Burglar for the mission of Thorin and Company. The hobbit will play a vital role in events that will culminate in *The Lord of the Rings*. He is destined to find the One Ring and pave the way for its destruction. To do his part, he must overcome his flaws and embrace the hero he was created to be.

———

To come full circle, then, what are we to make of the "humble hero" at the beginning of his book? Bilbo Baggins is not a bad person—not someone to be disliked, definitely not to be or ignored or shunned. Rather, he is pointedly unfinished. He is both the hero of the story and not yet heroic.

Fortunately, things began to change for Bilbo because of three life-altering words: "Gandalf came by."[4]

Speaking of Gandalf, there's another question to address concerning *The Hobbit*'s beginning. It's one most people are curious about when they start the story, although some think it's not supposed to be asked (or answered).

Namely, why would anyone—especially a wizard who seems to know what he's doing—choose *Bilbo* to participate in a dangerous quest?

Two observations will help us find the answer: (1) Gandalf specifically selected Bilbo, and (2) he made this choice based on outside information regarding the hobbit's inner character.

First, as the wizard affirms and confirms several times, starting here, he didn't run into Bilbo by accident; he intentionally chose Bilbo to join the venture. When they harp on his apparent lack of qualifications, Gandalf remains firm to the point of stern—daring the dwarves to accuse him of finding the "wrong man" and proposing that he leave the venture altogether if they don't like his choice.

What's more, soon thereafter he makes an intriguing declaration that there is more to him than you'd expect; more, even, than he's aware of himself.[5]

The message is plain: Gandalf was neither flippant nor foolish in tapping Bilbo for his task, and he had in no wise sought to hazard a fortunate guess. The wizard wanted Bilbo Baggins and only Bilbo Baggins. Gandalf knew that something inside Bilbo made him vital to the expedition's success—something of which even Bilbo himself wasn't yet aware.

Second, then: Gandalf was in possession of outside information.

Gandalf is a representative of Ilúvatar, divine Creator of Middle-earth. As such, he was present when Ilúvatar revealed a vision of what would happen in the world. And so he maintains a limited knowledge of future events, which is how he understood what the hobbit was really made of.

This necessarily impacts the way we view Bilbo's participation in the realm's larger events. He was not drafted by chance or by mistake into the battle between good and evil; rather, his inclusion was the result of a divine call. Before Ilúvatar shaped creation, he knew what would unfold there. Bilbo Baggins was formed in a specific way in order to accomplish a specific task, and in chapter 1 we see him being summoned to carry it out.

The same is true for us.

In his letter to the church at Ephesus, Paul begins by notifying the believers that their status as followers of Christ was not an accident or a turn of good luck but was divinely ordained:

Praise be to the God and Father of our Lord Jesus Christ, who has blessed us in the heavenly realms with every spiritual blessing in Christ. For he chose us in him before the creation of the world to be holy and blameless in his sight. In love he predestined us for adoption to sonship through Jesus Christ, in accordance with his pleasure and will.

Ephesians 1:3–5

We too are chosen with a preordained plan. Later Paul reminds them that they were not called to sit by in idle comfort and self-preserving safety; they were chosen so that one day they could stand and fight:

Finally, be strong in the Lord and in his mighty power. Put on the full armor of God, so that you can take your stand against the devil's schemes. For our struggle is not against flesh and blood, but against the rulers, against the authorities, against the powers of this dark world and against the spiritual forces of evil in the heavenly realms.

Therefore put on the full armor of God, so that when the day of evil comes, you may be able to stand your ground, and after you have done everything, to stand. Stand firm then, with the belt of truth buckled around your waist, with the breastplate of righteousness in place, and with your feet fitted with the readiness that comes from the gospel of peace.

In addition to all this, take up the shield of faith, with which you can extinguish all the flaming arrows of the evil one.

Take the helmet of salvation and the sword of the Spirit, which is the word of God.

Ephesians 6:10–17

In *The Hobbit*, Bilbo does stand and fight when the chips are down. In fact, he even picks up a few such weapons along the way. But his abilities and his courage take some time and some learning to develop.

Moral and Spiritual Growth

We've seen that *The Hobbit* was written with a strong theological basis. It is very much a Christian book because Tolkien was very much a Christian author. As you read it, one of the best places to see this foundation at work is within the theme of moral and spiritual growth.

One core concept of Christian doctrine is that human beings are born with a fatal flaw—something that's broken in the core of our beings must be fixed before we can become the people God created us to be. This defect is often defined as "sin" or our "sinful nature."

God is the one who ultimately fixes us, of course, and He does so in a dramatic way. Because of Jesus Christ's death and resurrection, we have the opportunity to be reborn. That is, we can be remade in such a way that our sin no longer prevents us from becoming who God intended.

Then, once the flaw has been removed, the rest of our lives become a journey of becoming our true selves—a process often referred to as "spiritual growth." The apostle Paul summarizes it this way:

> You were taught, with regard to your former way of life, to put off your old self, which is being corrupted by its deceitful desires; to be made new in the attitude of your minds; and to put on the new self, created to be like God in true righteousness and holiness.
>
> Ephesians 4:22–24

Here's the point: Tolkien intentionally built all of these ideas (and more) into the background and story of *The Hobbit*.

The affliction of Bilbo Baggins B.A. by his own flaw—that is, his incompleteness—results in the absence of certain virtues and the presence of certain vices. Throughout the rest of the story, Tolkien presents the hobbit with a series of opportunities to overcome that flaw and take another step toward becoming the hero he was created to be.

As we'll see in chapter 19, Bilbo's willingness to take advantage of these chances allows him in due course to shed his "old self" and "put on the new self." In other words, he becomes a new creation. He is born again.

Interestingly, Bilbo's opportunities for growth almost always involve some kind of hardship, another connection between *The Hobbit* and Christian doctrine. Scripture clarifies several times that believers often experience the most spiritual growth amid difficult circumstances. For example:

> Consider it pure joy, my brothers and sisters, whenever you face trials of many kinds, because you know that the testing of your faith produces perseverance. Let perseverance finish its work so that you may be mature and complete, not lacking anything.
>
> James 1:2–4

It's also important to note that Tolkien extends this pattern beyond Bilbo. Several characters are given opportunities for moral development. Some take advantage; others do not. Either way, their choices—and the spoils, or the consequences—are instructive.

Keeping this in mind, let's explore the beginning of Bilbo's journey toward maturity—and a few trolls along the way.

2

A Poor Beginning

Is there any experience more universal than failure? Whether the expectations are rooted in ourselves or in the people we care about, we all have felt the sting that comes from falling short of them. All of us too have suffered the shame and disgrace of having our failures immortalized in the memories of those who witnessed them.

Failure is so familiar in our society that we've churned out endless adages and maxims to help us deal with it: "If at first you don't succeed—try, try again"; "It's not whether you win or lose; it's how you play the game"; "What do you do when you fall off the horse? You get right back *on* it."

In chapter 2 of *The Hobbit*, Bilbo Baggins encounters his first prospect for moving away from his "old self" and beginning to live like the hero he's destined to become. And he fails miserably. Before the chapter comes to a close, he needs much more than a cheerful cliché or a trusty proverb to see him (and his friends) out of peril.

First, however, Bilbo faces another unavoidable reality: disappointment.

My Kingdom for a Pocket-Handkerchief!

Before Bilbo rushes away from his home and his hankies to meet the dwarves, something fascinating happens. (And no, it's not that he forgets to dust the mantelpiece.)

On the morning after the surprise party, he wakes up to an empty house. They and the wizard are gone, and at first Bilbo believes they've started their adventure without him. Shockingly, part of him is disappointed.

This is an important revelation. Tolkien once again emphasizes that Bilbo is *meant* to accompany the dwarves. He has been called; he has a job to do. Even more, Tolkien reminds us of that small, struggling seed of courage in Bilbo—that "Tookish" impulse awaiting the chance to be unleashed.

Of course, Bilbo does come to join the dwarves on their quest. At first, as it goes, he's pleased with the results—even to the point where he began to feel that adventures weren't so terrible after all.

Well, that feeling doesn't last long. The road gets bumpy. The weather turns dreary. Food begins to run short. And Bilbo starts to complain. He grumbles about the whole idea of burgling. He wishes longingly to be back in his nice hole by the fire, with his kettle just starting to sing—then the narrator interjects to let us know this "was not the last time that he wished that!"[1]

As you read *The Hobbit*, watch for those moments when Bilbo pines for the comfort and security of his safe little dwelling back in the Shire. These significant landmarks serve to keep reminding us that Bilbo is still a work in progress—that he has a lot of growing to do before becoming the hero of his own story.

Remember Paul's words from Ephesians 4:22–24:

> You were taught, with regard to your former way of life, to put off your old self, which is being corrupted by its deceitful desires; to be made new in the attitude of your minds; and to put on the new self, created to be like God in true righteousness and holiness.

When Bilbo longs for the comforting refuge of the Shire and Bag End, he really is refusing to "put off [his] old self" and work toward being "made new." Any of us who's honest will readily acknowledge that this negative response usually results in negative—and *un*comfortable—consequences.

That is certainly the case with the trolls.

A Poor Showing for "Burrahobbits"

Bilbo's encounter with the trolls Bert, Tom, and William is his first real experience with adventure. It does not go well.

To start, Bilbo is given a specific set of instructions. Thorin tells him to take a look at the fire they've spotted ahead and see if there's a problem or if everything is "safe and canny."[2] Either way, the hobbit is to report back quickly with news.

Naturally, things are neither safe nor canny. Bilbo discovers three trolls in a foul mood. But instead of updating Thorin, as directed, he attempts a little burglary. Not surprisingly, he is caught.

Perhaps this particular overzealousness can be forgiven,

as, after all, the hobbit joined this squad to be their burglar. But as for what happens after his capture . . .

First, he betrays the presence of the dwarves when a troll asks if anyone else is sneaking around in the woods. (Bilbo says, "Yes, lots.")[3]

Then, when the trolls begin to fight one another, Bilbo again forgoes the opportunity to flee in obeisance to his orders from Thorin. Instead, he remains on the ground, panting, because his poor little feet had been very squashed in the hands of the troll.

This pathetic scene is meant to be seen as pathetic. Though the hobbit has just escaped mortal danger, he's too tired to run away and save himself *or* to alert his friends.

Later still, as the trolls capture the dwarves one by one, Bilbo makes no attempt to rescue them. Worse, he makes no attempt even to *advise* them of the imminent menace— he merely stands behind a tree, watching it all go down. Only when Thorin appears does Bilbo cry out in warning and take a stab at helping. For his trouble, he is kicked into a bush; he then spends the rest of the skirmish "not daring to move for fear they should hear him."[4]

That is the key word for the entire incident: *fear*. Faced with impending risk, Bilbo is paralyzed in fright, just as he had frozen up back at his own house when the dwarves first informed him of their intentions—only this time their lives are in jeopardy.

"Be Strong and Courageous"

Bilbo's struggle with fear is another way his story reflects the process of spiritual growth in the believer's life.

Throughout God's Word, His followers are reminded again and again not to be rendered useless because of fear. Here are just a few examples:

Be strong and courageous. Do not be afraid or terrified because of them, for the Lord your God goes with you; he will never leave you nor forsake you.

Deuteronomy 31:6

I took you from the ends of the earth,
from its farthest corners I called you.
I said, "You are my servant";
I have chosen you and have not rejected you.
So do not fear, for I am with you;
do not be dismayed, for I am your God.
I will strengthen you and help you;
I will uphold you with my righteous right hand.

Isaiah 41:9–10

Who is going to harm you if you are eager to do good? But even if you should suffer for what is right, you are blessed. "Do not fear their threats; do not be frightened."

1 Peter 3:13–14

The thread of these commands is straightforward and easy enough to understand. Those who follow God are on the side of an everlasting, all-powerful, all-knowing, everywhere-present Being. Moreover, that Being loves us, cares for us, and desires only our good. More still, even if we should suffer in this lifetime, we know that our final destination is eternal life with Him in paradise. Therefore, we are never to be controlled by fear.

And yet, clear-cut, logical ideas are not always easy to carry out. This is certainly the case with fear—for hobbits *and* humans.

Focusing on chapter 2 of *The Hobbit*, the lesson to be learned is simple: at this point in the story, Bilbo is horrific at heroism. (He's not a very good burglar either.) He has a long, long way to go—in terms of both distance and development—before reaching that tunnel under the Lonely Mountain where he will make the most crucial choice of his life.

Lucky for Thorin and Company, Gandalf arrives in time to save the day.

Speaking of Gandalf, this is an excellent time for a deeper look into one of Tolkien's most popular characters—and inarguably the most mysterious.

Character Profile: Gandalf

J. R. R. Tolkien has long been recognized for wielding his phenomenal imagination on a grand scale. For Middle-earth he constructed a documented and detailed geography. He interwove diverse civilizations onto and over a historical platform. For the many races of beings within those civilizations, he created entire cultures, even formulating languages and mythologies for them.

But one area in which Tolkien is underappreciated regards his ability to originate and shape compelling characters within his stories—vital creatures who feel, who bleed, who err, who grow. That being the case, I will take opportunities throughout this book to highlight some of his more interesting creations, starting with Gandalf.

In order to plumb the depths of Gandalf as a character within *The Hobbit*, we will focus on two questions: who is he, and what is his role in the story?

Who Is Gandalf?

It's curious that, even though Gandalf plays a central role in this story, we as readers don't learn much more about him. In fact, here, essentially, is all we can say for certain after we turn the final page:

- He is a wizard and can do some magical things.
- He has been around a very long time.
- He is a member of the apparently important "council of the wise."[5]
- His wisdom and knowledge surpass that of others in the story.
- He is brave and compassionate but also demanding.
- He has a habit of showing up just in the nick of time.

Fortunately, Tolkien provided a few more details in his other books—especially in *The Silmarillion*.

For example, it's important to know that Gandalf is not a human being, not a man like Bard the Bowman or Aragorn. Rather, he is one of several immortal beings sent into the world as stewards at its very beginning.

As first noted in "A Short History of Middle-earth," these beings are split into two groups. The Valar—sometimes called the Lords of the West—are more powerful and are responsible for ruling the world. The Maiar serve the Valar in their divinely appointed stewardship. None of these are gods; they function similarly to how angels are perceived to function in our world, serving and representing the divine Creator.

> Gandalf, one of the Maiar, was originally called Olórin and is renowned for his wisdom and compassion. *The Silmarillion* records that during the realm's latter ages, he took special interest in the "Children of Ilúvatar" (elves and men).

Further, Gandalf is part of a unique group of Maiar—the Istari—re-sent to Middle-earth as representatives of Ilúvatar:

> Even as the first shadows were felt in Mirkwood there appeared in the west of Middle-earth the Istari, whom

Men call the Wizards. None knew at the time whence they were, save Cirdan of the Havens, and only to Elrond and Galadriel did he reveal that they came over the Sea. But afterwards it was said among the Elves that they were messengers sent by the Lords of the West to contest the power of Sauron, if he should rise again, and to move Elves and Men and all living things of good will to valiant deeds.[6]

Accordingly, one aspect of Gandalf's divinely appointed mission is to spur on "the Children of Ilúvatar" and "all living things of good will"—including hobbits!—to "valiant deeds."

We also know from Tolkien's other works that Gandalf has many names. He is called Mithrandir a few times in *The Lord of the Rings*, as well as Gandalf Stormcrow. He's also known as Tharkûn and Incanus.[7]

One other item of note: Gandalf is fallible. He is neither omniscient nor omnipotent, and he does make mistakes from time to time. It took him decades to realize Bilbo's ring was the One Ring, for instance, and in *The Hobbit* he inadvertently sends Bilbo and the dwarves on a bad path through Mirkwood. Also, chapter 6 reveals that Gandalf can be killed (more on that, if you wish, in *The Fellowship of the Ring*).

As a character, the marvelously deep and complex Gandalf becomes more so when we comprehend the many roles he plays in Middle-earth.

What Is Gandalf's Role in This Segment of the Story?

Again, Gandalf is an immortal being who was sent into Middle-earth on a divine mission. He is a representative of the Being who created the world, which makes him an angel-like agent of providence.

What exactly is providence? A distinction is usually made between "general providence," which refers to God's continually upholding the existence and natural order of the universe, and "special providence," which refers to God's extraordinary intervention in the lives of people. The latter variety in this story is demonstrated first through Gandalf and, later, through the eagles, through Beorn, and, in critical ways, through Bilbo.

Here Gandalf's special-providence role manifests in three distinct ways.

First, in *The Hobbit,* Gandalf is an Agent of Divine Initiation. With the possible exception of Sauron, Gandalf is the prime mover and shaker within Middle-earth. On Ilúvatar's behalf, he's the one initiating chains of events and setting in motion the wheels that drive history.

Though in connection with Bilbo's story, Gandalf performs this role on a smaller scale, the account still includes several examples. A short story called "The Quest of Erebor," published posthumously in *Unfinished Tales,* reveals that Gandalf nudged Thorin Oakenshield toward setting up an initiative to overthrow Smaug and regain the dwarves' lost treasure. (Gandalf had his own motives as well—he knew Smaug would be a powerful ally to Sauron if the dark wizard should ever return to power.)

In *The Hobbit* chapter 1 (and discussed also in "Quest of Erebor"), it's Gandalf who joins Bilbo to the venture, and of course this becomes vitally important later on. Not only does Bilbo play a pivotal role in the destruction of Smaug and many other evil creatures, he also finds the Ruling Ring. Along the journey to the Lonely Mountain, Gandalf enlists the help of other beings, including Gwaihir, Lord of the Eagles, and Beorn—both of whom provide invaluable assistance during the Battle of Five Armies.

Second, within *The Hobbit,* Gandalf is an Agent of Divine Rescue. The first time he assumes this function—in chapter 2, when the dwarves have been caught by trolls—surely is not his last arrival just in time to thwart disaster.

He rescues the dwarves (and Bilbo) from the Great Goblin after everyone is captured in the cave inside the Misty Mountains. He rescues the dwarves again by leading them from the tunnels back into daylight (Bilbo has to find his own way out of that one). Gandalf himself is technically rescued by the Lord of the Eagles once the goblins and wargs catch the company up a tree, but the quest is again saved when the wizard hatches an ingenious plan to befriend Beorn on the borders of Mirkwood.

Most of all, Gandalf arrives back at the last possible moment to rescue dwarves, elves, men, and a hobbit from the goblin hòrde's attack after Smaug is killed and the treasure becomes up for grabs.

Third, Gandalf is an Agent of Divine Wrath. This pattern can be observed throughout *The Hobbit* (as well as *The Lord of the Rings*): Whenever Gandalf comes in contact with the forces of evil, they rarely survive for long.

The trolls—Bert, Tom, and William—are first among those forces to face Gandalf's righteous anger and divine wrath. They are comical villains, yes, but he never flinches from ensuring their destruction. Next comes the Great Goblin, then several other goblins and wargs, and, ultimately, even Smaug was destroyed because of the plans and actions Gandalf commenced.

Literary Corner: Bilbo as a Divine Agent

As someone who loved great stories, Tolkien appreciated the ins and outs of great literature; he himself incorporated advanced literary techniques. One that pops up frequently is the use of foreshadowing—using present symbols or situations to point to a future event.

Chapter 2 offers an excellent example of foreshadowing during the incident with the trolls. Amid the action, we find all thirteen dwarves tied up in sacks and lain out on the ground. This image points toward three major events to come: (1) the dwarves trapped by the goblins at the tops of trees; (2) the dwarves (minus Thorin) cocooned in spider silk and hung from a branch; and (3) the dwarves packed into barrels and floated down the river.

We already know Gandalf comes to the rescue in chapter 2. But the trouble with Bert, Tom, and William also foreshadows Bilbo's eventual replacement (or complement) of Gandalf as an Agent of Providence.

We see him in his Agent roles later on and throughout the book: (1) Bilbo rescuing the dwarves from the spiders—Agent of Divine Rescue; (2) Bilbo leading the dwarves in killing a host of the spiders—Agent of Divine Wrath; (3) Bilbo formulating the plan to free the dwarves by packing them in barrels—Agent of Divine Initiation (and Rescue).

Here again is the central purpose Bilbo fulfills throughout the story. He has been called out to act as a representative of Providence, to serve the forces of good at work in the larger world, as Gandalf does. But at the end of chapter 2, he still is not ready for such a role.

He'll have plenty of chances to face his fear and begin his divinely appointed work when the company moves into the Misty Mountains. Fortunately, he is able first to rest with Elrond, in the Last Homely House.

3

An Old Friend

he third chapter is one of the shortest in *The Hobbit*, and little happens in terms of action or excitement. Still, there is much to be unpacked from Thorin and Company's stay in the Last Homely House—especially in reference to the history of the elves, and Elrond specifically, for his story is worth exploring.

First, however, I need to highlight another interesting glimpse into the mind and heart of Bilbo Baggins.

Not for the Last Time!

Remember when I said to keep an eye out for those moments when Bilbo pines for his hobbit-hole back in the Shire instead of focusing his energy on the tasks at hand? Well, take a look at the juxtaposition that occurs before and after Bilbo arrives at the house of Elrond.

The first glimpse into his thoughts comes several days after the incident with the trolls. As the company marches over a riverbank, they see the nearest edge of a large mountain chain in the distance. Bilbo mistakenly believes this to be the Lonely Mountain—the end of their quest—and asks Balin about it. The dwarf scoffs and informs Bilbo that the journey has only just begun.

Bilbo is beyond disappointed. Like a child yelling "Are we there yet?" from the backseat, Bilbo is devastated to learn that the company has plenty of journey ahead. He thinks of his comfortable chair in front of the fire. He thinks of his favorite sitting-room in his hobbit-hole. He thinks of the kettle singing—and all of it "Not for the last time!"[1]

This sort of rubbernecking reminds us of Jesus' words in Luke 9:62: "No one who puts a hand to the plow and looks back is fit for service in the kingdom of God." Again, Tolkien is making sure we see that Bilbo really is a beginner in terms of his development; he is not yet fit for service.

But something unexpected happens when he and his friends finally meet Elrond and the elves in the Last Homely House. For a moment, at least, the Shire is all but forgotten. Bilbo thinks he could gladly remain in that house forever and ever—he even surprises himself by noting he would prefer to remain in Elrond's house even if a wish would carry him straight back to his hobbit-hole in the Shire.

Quite a change in attitude! And the reason is simple: In Elrond's home, Bilbo gets to experience all the enjoyable dimensions of adventure—elves, songs, stories, food, runes, maps, and more—without any of the danger.

In other words, here Bilbo has a "mountaintop experience," like Jesus' disciples had on the Mount of Transfiguration:

Jesus took with him Peter, James and John the brother of James, and led them up a high mountain by themselves. There he was transfigured before them. His face shone like the sun, and his clothes became as white as the light. Just then there appeared before them Moses and Elijah, talking with Jesus.

Peter said to Jesus, "Lord, it is good for us to be here. If you wish, I will put up three shelters—one for you, one for Moses and one for Elijah."

Matthew 17:1–4

Peter was thrilled to be in the presence of a glorified Jesus, not to mention Moses and Elijah—heroes of his Jewish faith and culture. This was so amazing that he wanted to build tents and keep the party going indefinitely.

Jesus had other plans for them. His followers had to travel a long and difficult road before they could accomplish great things for His kingdom.

The same will be true for Bilbo.

Character Profile: Elrond

If any Tolkien character were to receive the award for "Best Introduction," it would be Elrond Half-Elven. The narrator describes him as an amalgam of the best traits found in elf-lords, warriors, wizards, kings of the dwarves—*and* he's "as kind as summer."[2] Not bad!

To shed some more light on Elrond, I'll briefly explain his history in Tolkien's larger world, then add some insights about his role in *The Hobbit*.

WHO IS ELROND?

The reason Tolkien gives Elrond such sublime description has to do with his extensive and complicated lineage.

To get a handle on Elrond's parentage, we need to start with his father, Eärendil. As I mentioned in "A Short History of Middle-Earth," Eärendil was the son of a human father, Tuor, and an elf mother, Idril. Tuor was one of the mightiest warriors ever seen in Middle-earth; Idril was a princess in Gondolin, fairest of the elf kingdoms established in Middle-earth.

Elrond could trace his roots to both the high elves of the West and one of the lords of humankind—and that's just on his father's side.

Elrond's mother, Elwing, was a descendant of Beren and Luthién—another marriage between man and elf. Beren also was a mighty warrior, and Luthién was "the most beautiful of all the Children of Ilúvatar."[3] Together, Beren and Luthién broke through the gates of Angband and stole a Silmaril from the iron crown of Melkor. (Eärendil carried this same Silmaril when he sailed west to seek the Valar's help against Melkor.)

And that's not all.

Luthién was the daughter of Thingol and Melian, another mixed marriage—although this time not between elf and man. Thingol was an elf, but Melian was a Maiar. Like Gandalf, she was an immortal being who took part in the creation of the world and committed to serving in it as a steward.

Thus, Elrond is a descendant of elves, men, *and* the world's angelic stewards. In many ways, he represents a combination (and a distillation) of the best Middle-earth has to offer.

At the end of the first age, the children of Eärendil and Elwing were given a choice by the Valar: they could be counted among the kindred either of elves or of men, but not both. Elrond's brother, Elros, chose to be counted among men, and he was the first king of the Númenórians.

Elrond chose to be counted among the elves, and he lived in Middle-earth. Not surprisingly, he was a major player in the events that unfolded there in his lifetime.

Elrond was the herald of Gil-Galad, one of the Noldor and the last king of the elves in Middle-earth. In that role, Elrond took part in the wars against Sauron. He helped form the last alliance between elves and men, and he was present when Isildur slashed the Ruling Ring from Sauron's finger.

Afterward, Elrond maintained a strong bond with the remnants of the Númenórians in Gondor. He gave shelter and council to the descendents of Isildur, Gondor's rightful rulers, even to the point of serving as a foster parent to Aragorn after his father died.

Elrond was a leading member of the White Council that tracked Sauron's movements after the Shadow began creeping back into the world, and it was Elrond who called the council that would determine that Frodo should take the One Ring to Mordor and destroy it in the fires of Mount Doom.

When Elrond (accompanied by Bilbo and Frodo) left Middle-earth to sail into the West at the end of *The Lord of the Rings*, he was more than six thousand years old. In every way, he represented the best of the forces of good in Middle-earth and beyond.

What Is Elrond's Role in This Segment of the Story?

As with Gandalf, Elrond takes on a more subdued role in *The Hobbit*.

On a practical level, he provides Thorin and Company much-needed rest after their first burst of adventure in the wild. His finding the moon-letters on Thorin's map proves vital once the travelers reach the Lonely Mountain.

But the main reasons for Elrond's inclusion in the story are more subtle: (1) He provides a connection to the larger history of Middle-earth, and (2) he represents a compelling contrast to Bilbo.

First, Elrond is a living legend, and his presence within *The Hobbit* serves to connect Bilbo's story with the larger mythology Tolkien always had in mind—and to forge a connection between Bilbo's adventure and the world's larger conflict between good and evil.

Indeed, the narrator links Elrond with the struggles of the Valar against Melkor before the planting of the Two Trees of Valinor, which began the keeping of Time. Elrond was also part of the thousands of years of conflict between the high elves and the servants of Melkor. And the fact that Elrond has both elves and heroes of the North for ancestors stirs up echoes of Tuor, Eärendil, Elwing, Beren, Luthién, and many others.

Elrond yields another historical link when he reveals the history of the swords Gandalf and Thorin took from the trolls. They came from Gondolin, which someone connected to Middle-earth's history would automatically associate with sorrow and loss. Gondolin was the fairest kingdom of the elves in Middle-earth—until it was destroyed by Melkor's creatures through a jealous elf's treachery.

In *The Hobbit*, Gandalf and Thorin (and later, Bilbo), carrying blades made during the height of Gondolin's power, forge connections across time in highlighting the struggle of good against evil.

One more fascinating piece of information about Gondolin's fall: This was the first narrative element Tolkien wrote in his larger mythology. He was twenty-three at the time and in a military hospital after the Battle of the Somme. Originally called "Tuor and the Exiles of Gondolin," this story reflected his own personal experiences with the ongoing struggle between good and evil.[4]

SHAMING THE WISE

The second reason for Elrond's inclusion—providing a point of contrast with Bilbo—emphasizes that Providence often chooses to work through weakness rather than strength.

After all, wouldn't Elrond have made an amazing protagonist on the basis of his lineage and past accomplishments? He is a bona fide hero—an immortal being filled with power and wisdom who millennium after millennium has opposed the forces of evil.

Wouldn't it have made more sense for Tolkien to write *The Half-Elven* than *The Hobbit*?

But Tolkien chose a different path—a different hero. And he did so because he wanted his story to reflect a primary truth made clear in the Bible: God reveals His strength by working through the weakest of vessels.

Look at these words from Paul, for example:

Brothers and sisters, think of what you were when you were called. Not many of you were wise by human standards; not many were influential; not many were of noble birth. But God chose the foolish things of the world to shame the wise; God chose the weak things of the world to shame the strong.

1 Corinthians 1:26–27

We have this treasure in jars of clay to show that this all-surpassing power is from God and not from us. We are hard pressed on every side, but not crushed; perplexed, but not in despair; persecuted, but not abandoned; struck down, but not destroyed.

2 Corinthians 4:7–9

Here's what can be said of Bilbo at the end of chapter 3: He's a weak vessel, a jar of clay. He is a non-heroic hobbit who, hopefully, is in the process of becoming the hero he was created to be. And he must progress in this transformation because he has been drafted into the most ancient of struggles. And more than drafted—he has a vital part to play.

It all really gets started in a tunnel under the Misty Mountains when nobody else is around to help.

4

Darkness and Light

In many ways, chapter 4 is where the *adventure* part of Bilbo's adventure truly gets started. Yes, the journey from the Shire to the borderlands was uncomfortable. And yes, the business with the trolls was unfortunate.

But the early parts of Bilbo's story do not carry a sense of true peril until the goblins get involved. That's the first time we begin to feel the tension of potentially lethal consequences. Down in the tunnels beneath the mountains, with hordes of furious goblins shrieking and chasing Thorin and Company, we begin to think even Gandalf will have to work some serious magic to come through alive.

So how will poor, easily terrified Bilbo handle the situation?

Baby Steps

My grandson Brogan is taking his first steps; it's a very up-and-down experience. On the one hand, the steps themselves are nothing to write home about. The child stumbles forward a few paces, wobbles, loses his balance, stumbles a bit more, then falls into his mother's arms.

On the other hand, they're a landmark accomplishment. They are his *first steps*! They're a definitive sign that he is moving out of one development stage and starting another. And they're a sign that, in time, he will master the skill of walking and adopt a whole new method of moving around.

That's basically what happens in Bilbo's first encounter with the goblins.

After Thorin and Company escape from the storm and take refuge in a small cave, everyone, including the hobbit, goes to sleep. But Bilbo doesn't sleep peacefully. He dreams that a crack opens in the back of the wall, and the floor of the cave tilts upward so that he begins sliding toward the blackness.

When he wakes, he finds that part of his dream has come true: a door has opened up in the cave's back, and he sees the tails of their ponies disappearing into it. In response, he yells.

On the one hand, Bilbo's actions can't really be considered heroic. He woke up, he saw something, and he yelled. Anyone could do that, right?

On the other hand, what's significant about this incident is that *Bilbo does something*. He takes action! During his previous encounters with danger, he was paralyzed by fear. In chapter 1, he was thrown into paroxysms of terror by the imagined presence of a dragon. And when the trolls hid themselves in the woods to capture the dwarves one by one, Bilbo, controlled by dread, did absolutely nothing to warn his friends.

This time, however, Bilbo does give a warning. And not just a frightened croak—he gives as loud a yell as a hobbit is able to give—and we're told that hobbits are indeed able to create a surprising amount of noise for their size. In other words, Bilbo gave his best effort.

Small step, but a positive one, and it represents bigger things to come.

Here's another interesting tidbit: Tolkien makes it a point to mention that even Gandalf may have been in trouble had it not been for Bilbo. The hobbit's cry woke the wizard, and so he was able to kill several goblins with a flash, thereby evading capture.

This shows that Bilbo was now working as part of Gandalf's team. He was contributing to the cause rather than passively standing by. Like Gandalf, Bilbo was now serving as an Agent of Divine Rescue.

Literary Corner: Flames of Wrath

Speaking of Gandalf, I want to highlight one of Tolkien's more effective uses of symbolism in *The Hobbit*.

I mentioned earlier that within the story, Gandalf functions as an Agent of Divine Wrath—he's a storm of righteous anger against the forces of evil. This can be seen clearly in his treatment of the goblins. From the moment several of these creatures try to seize the wizard in the cave, all the way up to their attempted ambush in the tunnels below, Gandalf slays them without mercy.

One of the destructive tools he uses, the sword Glamdring, also functions as a symbol of the wizard's divine wrath. We see this for the first time when the sword flashes with its own light as it slays the Great Goblin.

Tolkien explains that Glamdring burned with a rage causing it to glow whenever goblins are about. He also alerts us that the sword gleamed with bright blue flame for delight in the destruction of the Great Goblin.

Swords aren't conscious beings, of course—even in this particular fairy story. But Glamdring's blue fire is a visual representation of Gandalf's righteous anger, and of the triumph of light over darkness. The same can be said of Thorin's sword, Orcrist, which also burns with an inner light in the presence of evil creatures. (And of Bilbo's little sword, Sting, as we'll see.)

Actually, all of Gandalf's attacks on the goblins involve some form of fire or flame. He kills the first ones with "a terrific flash like lightning."[1] When the Great Goblin attacks Thorin, Gandalf sends up a tower of blue glowing smoke that scatters piercing white sparks down onto the goblins. He uses Glamdring with its blue fire against the Great Goblin and several others. And in chapter 6, when Gandalf and the dwarves are trapped in trees by the wargs, the wizard lights pinecones with a magic fire and throws them down to set the wolves aflame.

Believe it or not, this symbolism is straight from the Bible.

In the ancient world, fire was often associated with divinity. (Think of Prometheus, of Greek mythology—he stole fire from Zeus and brought it to humankind.) This connection was regularly incorporated by the authors of Scripture, who used fire as a symbol for the one true God.

Here are a few examples:

> How long, Lord? Will you hide yourself forever?
> How long will your wrath burn like fire?
>
> Psalm 89:46 (one of several
> instances in the Psalms)

82

I saw that from what appeared to be his waist up he looked like glowing metal, as if full of fire, and that from there down he looked like fire; and brilliant light surrounded him.

Ezekiel 1:27 (from the prophet's vision of God)

The hair on his head was white like wool, as white as snow, and his eyes were like blazing fire.

Revelation 1:14 (from John's vision of Jesus)

And of course, the clearest connection comes near the Bible's beginning:

After he drove the man out, he placed on the east side of the Garden of Eden cherubim and a flaming sword flashing back and forth to guard the way to the tree of life.

Genesis 3:24

This is yet another intentional link Tolkien forged between his Christian beliefs and his sub-created realm. He took a symbolic element that's common in the Scriptures and used it as a building material for his Secondary World.

Character Profile: The Goblins

Every good story needs a villain, and for most of *The Hobbit*, it seems Smaug the dragon will serve as primary antagonist. When all is said and done, however, it's the hordes of hideous goblins (also called orcs) that prove the biggest threat to the forces of good in Middle-earth.

Incidentally, the same is true in *The Lord of the Rings*. While the Black Riders, Shelob the spider, and other creatures do make things uncomfortable for Frodo and the champions of good, it's the vicious legions of goblins at Sauron's command that collectively make victory seem impossible until the very last moment.

So let's take a minute to explore (1) the history of the goblins in Tolkien's world, and (2) their specific role in Bilbo's adventure.

The History of the Goblins

Genesis 1 makes plain that everything God made was originally good. There were no flaws until sin entered the world to bring chaos and destruction. One of the main principles we can glean from these assertions is that nothing was created to be evil. Evil exists only as a distortion of what used to be good.

While the circumstances are a bit different in Middle-earth—the world's genesis was knocked askew earlier in the process, when Melkor's self-will disrupted the song of creation—Tolkien clearly follows the scriptural template for sin and malevolence. In his world too, evil exists only as a corruption or privation of something that was once good.

The goblins are probably the best example of this principle in action.

The Silmarillion provides the clearest details on how they were brought into being, telling us that the forefathers of all the orcs/goblins in Middle-earth were actually elves—beings of light twisted and corrupted by Melkor over generations until they became servants of darkness.

I like Tolkien's choice of words in describing this process: the "Orcs [were made] in envy and mockery of the Elves." That's an excellent depiction of how evil operates in our world, both in Scripture and in everyday life.

The Goblins' Role in This Segment of the Story

The goblins serve a few purposes in Bilbo's story, some more obvious than others.

At the most basic level, goblins are evil's primary foot-soldiers. This is quickly made apparent by their actions, but Tolkien also highlights their evil nature through the imagery of light and dark: The goblins live in tunnels under the mountains, they can see well in pitch-darkness, and they don't like the sun.

This imagery, which continues throughout *The Hobbit*, is also a primary theme in Tolkien's other works. As you read, keep an eye out for other creatures that dwell in darkness, and especially for the times when Bilbo and his friends are forced to endure long periods of time without the light of day.

Of course, this contrast is used regularly in Scripture to represent the disparity between good and evil. Here are just a few examples:

> Praise be to the name of God for ever and ever;
> wisdom and power are his. . . .
> He reveals deep and hidden things;
> he knows what lies in darkness,
> and light dwells with him.
>
> Daniel 2:20, 22

> Your eye is the lamp of your body. When your eyes are healthy, your whole body also is full of light. But when they are unhealthy, your body also is full of darkness.
>
> Luke 11:34

> This is the verdict: Light has come into the world, but people loved darkness instead of light because their deeds were evil.
>
> John 3:19

On a deeper level, Tolkien's goblins reflect humanity's capacity for destruction—especially our ability to destroy *en masse*, that is, to destroy each other as well as the world around us, through industrialization and technology.

The narrator informs us that goblins are cruel and bad-hearted. They don't make any lovely or beautiful things, although they do make many clever ones. In fact, we're told that the goblins probably invented many of the machines and engines now troubling the world—especially those ingenious devices able to kill large numbers of people at once.

Remember that Tolkien wasn't writing an allegory, so the goblins are not personifications of industrialization or the horrors of armed conflict. Rather, they are sub-creations that Tolkien intended to be evil. Therefore, he gave them characteristics that matched what he considered to be evil in the world around him.

When considering this point, recall that Tolkien was involved with *The Silmarillion* after the mass carnage of World War I; he also finished writing *The Hobbit* on the brink of World War II, and *The Lord of the Rings* trilogy after the advent of the atomic bomb. More, he was a lover of trees and flowers and the unspoiled beauty of nature. It's no surprise, then, that the evil species in his stories should be connected to bombs, tanks, and other "advances" able to transform a beloved countryside into muddy trenches and dead bodies.

The Good Part of Evil

You're probably familiar with the term *oxymoron*. This figure of speech combines two words or ideas that, at first glance, are contradictory. "Jumbo shrimp" is a common example. So is "passive-aggression" and "freezer burn."

Though not a strict oxymoron, here's another to consider: "good out of evil." Doesn't that sound rather silly at first? But it's a doctrine straight from the pages of Scripture.

The Bible has a lot to say about God's sovereignty (although it doesn't always use that word). God not only created the universe, but He is in control over all that happens in it. He is sovereign over everything—including evil.

That's one of the ideas He communicated through the prophet Isaiah:

> I am the Lord,
> and there is no other.
> I form the light and create darkness,
> I bring prosperity and create disaster;
> I, the Lord, do all these things.
>
> Isaiah 45:6–7

This is one of the themes present in Job's inspiring story:

> His wife said to him, "Are you still maintaining your integrity? Curse God and die!"
> He replied, "You are talking like a foolish woman. Shall we accept good from God, and not trouble?"
>
> Job 2:9–10

It's not just that God is aware of evil and has the power to stop it if He chooses. Both are true, but what the Bible also makes clear is that God views evil in the world as another tool He can utilize to accomplish His purposes.

That's what Joseph wanted his brothers to understand when they were feeling distraught about selling him into a life of slavery:

> Don't be afraid. Am I in the place of God? You intended to harm me, but God intended it for good to accomplish what is now being done, the saving of many lives. So then, don't be afraid. I will provide for you and your children.
>
> Genesis 50:19–21

That's also what Paul makes plain in Romans 8:28: "We know that in all things God works for the good of those who love him, who have been called according to his purpose."

Tolkien was highly appreciative of this reality, which is oft-reflected throughout his many stories—starting with *The Silmarillion* creation account:

> Then Ilúvatar spoke, and he said: "Mighty are the Ainur, and mightiest among them is Melkor; but that he may know, and all the Ainur, that I am Ilúvatar, those things that ye have sung, I will show them forth, that ye may see what ye have done. And thou, Melkor, shalt see that no theme may be played that hath not its uttermost source in me, nor can any alter the music in my despite. For he that attempteth this shall prove but mine instrument in the devising of things more wonderful, which he himself hath not imagined."[2]

This idea that Providence can weave evil actions into the song of good is also present in *The Hobbit*, most visibly with the goblins. In fact, the goblins reflect this pattern in at least three distinct ways.

First, the goblins produce suffering. This makes sense, of course, for evil actions often produce suffering. But remember that both *The Hobbit* and the Bible view suffering as one of the best ways to experience moral and spiritual growth (see chapter 1 of Part II). If Bilbo hadn't suffered at goblin hands, he would not have been prepared to face the spiders in Mirkwood. And if he had not faced the spiders, he would not have been prepared to face Smaug.

Second, the goblins force a change in plan. Evil actions often produce unintended consequences. Again, one example would be spiritual growth. But the presence of evil in the world can also compel people to make decisions they wouldn't otherwise choose to make. For example, many people returned to church and renewed their faith in Christ after the 9/11 terrorist attacks.

In *The Hobbit*, the goblins' actions under the Misty Mountains and in the forest beyond forced Gandalf to seek help from the eagles and from Bard the Bowman. Both became critical pieces in the victory over the goblins in the Battle of Five Armies.

Third, the goblins initiated their own doom. One of the most compelling themes in *The Lord of the Rings* is that evil is self-destructive—the evil actions of evil beings ultimately brings about the destruction of those beings. This is true in *The Hobbit* as well. For instance, the Great Goblin's scheme of waylaying travelers in the mountain eventually produces his demise when he attempts to snare Gandalf.

In these ways and more, the Creator can be appropriate evil to accomplish good. We will see all three taking place in chapter 5.

5

Turning Points

People's lives are usually filled with mostly normal moments—regular routines and patterns we repeat day in and day out. Every now and then an important moment comes along, although it's not a given that we'll recognize it. And if we do recognize it, there's no guarantee we'll make the adjustments necessary to take advantage of it.

On the rarest of occasions, a person may be presented with something totally different—a moment filled with life-changing, world-shaking potential. Moses noticing a burning bush would be a good example, or Pilate deciding to wash his hands of the problem posed by a certain carpenter from Nazareth.

At the beginning of *The Hobbit* chapter 5, Bilbo Baggins is about to stumble onto one of those moments. I'll take a step back and set the scene a little bit. Gandalf was able to rescue Bilbo and the dwarves from the goblins, but the company was attacked from behind while attempting to navigate the labyrinthine tunnels under the Misty Mountains. Bilbo, knocked unconscious in the assault, fell senseless into a dark corner—unnoticed by goblins or dwarves or even wizards.

When Bilbo woke some time later, he was alone. He guessed which way Gandalf might have been heading, and started to crawl . . . and that's when his hand met a "tiny ring of cold metal."[1] This is not just any ring. It's the One Ring—the Ruling Ring that Sauron created as part of his plan to dominate all life in Middle-earth.

The ring had been missing for *thousands* of years; its rediscovery would initiate all the events in *The Lord of the Rings*.

Talk about a turning point!

Of course, it will be a long time before anyone begins to suspect the import of this find. For Bilbo, alone in the darkness, with no way of escape, the ring means nothing. He puts it in his pocket and moves on without a second thought.

The chapter's beginning contains a second turning point more relevant to Bilbo's immediate scenario: a giant leap forward in his struggle against fear.

Moving Forward

The situation that precedes this turning point is particularly grim. For one thing, Bilbo has no idea where he is and no idea how to escape. He can't see, he has no food, he can't even comfort himself with a quick pull on his pipe.

Most poignantly, Bilbo has no Gandalf. There is no one to rescue him or fight against his enemies—not even a dwarf. He is alone.

Given those facts, and based on what we've seen from Mr. Baggins so far along the way, it would be reasonable to assume he'd curl into a ball and tremble with fright until the goblins found him. And initially, he does start out by longing for bacon and eggs back in his own kitchen, and he does search his pockets for tobacco, his pipe, some matches—all relics of security.

Again, this is Bilbo pining for the Shire and his old way of life—his "old self." However, on the brink of that longing, something unexpected happens that helps the hobbit lurch toward becoming a new creation: He sees the light.

Hunting for matches, he instead finds the little sword he had taken from the trolls' lair—and to his surprise, it glows with a pale flame, just as Gandalf's does. Bilbo realizes that his blade also came out of Gondolin, and he's encouraged by the thought. He even seems a little more courageous.

What's happening here?

First, on a practical level, Bilbo is comforted to have a source of light so that he can see in the darkness. Having a weapon likewise makes him feel more secure about the goblins. These legitimate reactions make perfect sense—but they don't tell the whole story of this crucial moment in his life.

There is a second, deeper level at play. Namely, Bilbo is starting to become who he was created to be. Remember the unexpected vision he had during the unexpected party, back in chapter 1 of this section? When something Tookish awakened inside him?

Just look at him now! He's under the great mountains; he arrived there through a cave (though it'd be a stretch to say he was "exploring" anything); he's now wearing his own sword. Bilbo Baggins, previously described as more like a grocer than a burglar, has begun to realize his secret dreams.

Speaking of that sword, observe how, in another key application of concrete imagery, Tolkien emphasizes that its light is pale and dim. Last chapter, I noted how the blue flame of Gandalf's sword was connected with divine wrath. Here, the light of Bilbo's sword is more diminished—a gentle reminder of divine presence. The hobbit is in a tough spot, but Providence is with him to light the way.

That vivid illustration calls to mind this assurance: "Your word is a lamp for my feet, a light on my path" (Psalm 119:105).

Realize also that the sword immediately connects Bilbo with the larger history of the world. He's proud to be wearing a sword made in Gondolin for the goblin wars, and he recalls songs he used to hear sung about brave deeds in those times. This is Tolkien's way of reminding us that the war between good and evil has been raging for millennia, and that Bilbo has been drafted into it—though of course he doesn't realize that, having found the One Ring, he'll soon become the subject of many songs himself.

Now, for the first time, Bilbo Baggins demonstrates pure, unadulterated courage in the face of fear and doubt when he decides to move forward through the tunnel. The same hobbit who was unable to run from the trolls because his feet were squashed charges forward into the depths of an orc-infested tunnel without a contrary thought.

Bilbo is changed. He has grown. He's becoming who he was made to be.

The One Ring

When I talk with others about J. R. R. Tolkien and his work, there's one subject that causes more confusion and more wild theorizing than any other: the One Ring. People want to know what it represents—what it means.

There *are* certainly a lot of theories. Some, for instance, have speculated that the ring is an allegorical representation of evil or technology. Others hypothesize that the ring represents power of any kind and that Tolkien was making a point about absolute power corrupting absolutely.

To obtain a proper understanding of the Ruling Ring, we must remember that Tolkien was not a fan of such allegorical connections. Rather than having Gandalf represent the Holy Spirit or the One Ring represent absolute power, Tolkien simply wanted to fashion a Secondary World filled with cultures and characters who behaved in a realistic way to create stories.

Now, because Tolkien created this realm, using the same foundations and principles God used to create our Primary World, there are many similarities and connections between Middle-earth and Earth—some of which I have mentioned. For Tolkien, however, in this medium, the story always trumped any effort to push a message or make a statement.

Therefore, the One Ring doesn't *mean* anything outside of its place in Tolkien's mythology.

THE BEGINNING OF THE RINGS

To discover how Tolkien intended the ring to function within his story, let's go back to *The Silmarillion*. After Melkor was recaptured by the Valar and banished from the world, Sauron took on a pleasing form and made contact with the remaining elves and men in Middle-earth. He called himself Annatar, "the Lord of Gifts," and he traveled far and wide, teaching and giving gifts of knowledge. One of these gifts was the ability to create rings of power.

Sauron would give rings to elves, men, and dwarves with surreptitious intent to control their thoughts and actions using the One (or Ruling) Ring. Eventually he was exposed, but not before snaring several ring-bearers into his service, including the nine men who became the Nazgûl, known also as the Black Riders.

The One Ring was an exceedingly powerful object designed to subdue and control other powerful objects. That it contained "much of the strength and will of Sauron" in many ways made it an extension of him. Thus, the ring is powerful because Sauron poured his power into it; the ring is evil because Sauron poured his evil into it; and the ring corrupts those who use it because it contains Sauron's will to control all other life.

Oh, and it shares some commonalities with the other rings of power—like, for instance, turning people invisible.

LITERARY CORNER: THE WILL OF THE RING

I want to quickly highlight a technique Tolkien uses to show the separated will and malice possessed by the One Ring.

Remember when Gollum suspects that Bilbo has the ring in his pocket and chases after the hobbit with the intent to commit murder? When Bilbo runs for it, notice the inverted phrasing Tolkien uses to describe what happens next: As Bilbo puts his hand in his pocket, "the ring felt very cold as it quietly slipped on to his groping forefinger."[2]

Did you catch that? Not "Bilbo slipped the ring onto his finger," but "the ring felt very cold as it quietly *slipped onto* his groping forefinger." The *ring* performs the action as if it is a thing alive.

While this might be discounted as coincidence if it happened once, remember Gollum. While searching for Bilbo, he realizes the ring must have become lost when he attacked a young goblin in the tunnel. "Curse it!" he says. "It slipped from us, after all these ages and ages."[3]

Bilbo himself has a similar revelation when he realizes the goblins at the back door can see him—the ring isn't on his finger. Then, when Bilbo puts a hand in his pocket to check for the ring, the ring slips back on his finger.

The *ring* slipped from Gollum. The *ring* took a new master. The *ring* slipped onto Bilbo's finger. The active language shows us that the ring possesses a will and a malice of its own.

A Pity?

In a chapter filled with turning points, there is one last event to address. This happens when Bilbo contemplates killing Gollum in order to reach the back door and escape into the sunlight.

Bilbo is desperate to escape from the tunnels with their horrible darkness. He thinks he must put Gollum's eyes out and then kill it—it meant to kill him, after all.

But then something changes. He sees that it's no longer a fair fight since he is invisible and Gollum is defenseless, and he begins to feel pity for this poor, miserable creature.

This decisive crossroads is as vital to the well-being of Middle-earth as Bilbo's finding of the Ruling Ring or Frodo's choice to carry it to Mordor. Without Gollum, the ring would never have been destroyed at the end of the story.

Gandalf hints at this reality at the beginning of *The Fellowship of the Ring*, the first volume in *The Lord of the Rings*. When Frodo expresses regret that Bilbo did not kill Gollum in the moment described above, Gandalf responds with a mild rebuke, telling him that the pity Bilbo showed Gollum was honorable. In *The Hobbit*, Bilbo does not start out with an unending supply of heroism and courage, but he does possess an inherent goodness—a deep measure of virtue, of mercy and compassion. That those qualities do not diminish as his courage grows seals the ultimate fate of Middle-earth.

This emphasis is another infusion into Tolkien's Secondary World of scriptural values and principles. Consider these passages, for example:

> The Lord our God is merciful and forgiving, even though we have rebelled against him.
>
> Daniel 9:9

But a Samaritan, as he traveled, came where the man was; and when he saw him, he took pity on him. He went to him and bandaged his wounds, pouring on oil and wine. Then he put the man on his own donkey, brought him to an inn and took care of him.

Luke 10:33–34

Speak and act as those who are going to be judged by the law that gives freedom, because judgment without mercy will be shown to anyone who has not been merciful. Mercy triumphs over judgment.

James 2:12–13

This brings up an interesting question: If Bilbo will come to replace Gandalf as an Agent of Divine Wrath, why should he have shown pity at all? Would it not have been better for the hobbit to slay Gollum in a burst of righteous anger in the same way that the wizard slew the goblins?

The answer would be yes if Gollum were wholly evil, as were the orcs. But there seems to be some debate on this point.

In the same discussion with Frodo from *The Fellowship of the Ring*, Gandalf several times mentions that Gollum may not be wholly corrupted. He even holds open the possibility for redemption, saying: "I have not much hope that Gollum can be cured before he dies, but there is a chance of it."[4]

Bilbo also senses this small hope. Confronted by the creature in a helpless state, Bilbo is struck by an understanding of Gollum's hopeless situation. In the end, this comprehension is enough cause for Bilbo to choose life over death, mercy over judgment. His choice preserves the future of Middle-earth.

6

Two Escapes

"He who fights and runs away lives to fight another day."
That's an old saying, and one not often used in connection with heroic characters (or those supposed to be heroic characters). Even so, the ability to escape from trouble is an important attribute for Gandalf and his friends in chapter 6 of *The Hobbit*.

In fact, this chapter features two escapes—the first of which is extremely subtle, while the second is almost too obvious and convenient.

Carefully and Quietly

After Bilbo escapes through the back door of the goblins' lair and out into the sunshine, he has the good fortune to quickly stumble upon his friends. They're overjoyed to see him, and they want to know how he could have done it.

But that's when something odd happens. For the first time in the story, Bilbo is intentionally dishonest. Mentioning nothing about the ring, instead he insists he made his way out simply by creeping along "very carefully and quietly."[1] He tells this lie twice, in direct succession—bang, bang.

What are we to make of this sudden turn? Bilbo Baggins, who couldn't even be dishonest with three trolls, is now lying to his friends? To Gandalf?

The unfortunate truth is that the One Ring's corrupting power already has begun its work on the hobbit. And in truth, the lies were not the first clue that the ring had taken hold. Back in chapter 5, when he noticed that the ring had slipped from his finger, he felt a loss similar to Gollum's own misery.

The malicious and corruptive will of this ring even then had formed a connection with him. And this was a terrible bond for someone like Bilbo—someone who'd been struggling to move away from selfishness and cowardice toward nobility and courage.

Strangely, though, this initial connection and subsequent burst of deception is as far as the ring seems to go in *The Hobbit*. There is no more "slipping" off and on, no more uncharacteristically unscrupulous behavior. Once the ring grabs hold of Bilbo, it doesn't seem to make further inroads in terms of his personal corruption.

Why? What is it about Bilbo that allowed him to escape its deadly influence?

Characteristically, Gandalf has some answers. The first has to do with Bilbo's actions during his first experience wearing the ring. He tells Frodo:

Be sure that [Bilbo] took so little hurt from the evil, and escaped in the end, because he began his ownership of the Ring so. With pity.[2]

Gandalf was referring to Bilbo's refusal to kill Gollum when he had the chance. He showed compassion and had mercy, and his act of virtue somehow protected the hobbit from much of the ring's initial onslaught.

But there's another reason the ring has so little influence on Bilbo throughout the course of *The Hobbit*, and Gandalf mentions it earlier in that same conversation:

So now, when its master was awake once more and sending out his dark thought from Mirkwood, [the ring] abandoned Gollum. Only to be picked up by the most unlikely person imaginable: Bilbo from the Shire!

Behind that there was something else at work, beyond any design of the Ring-maker. I can put it no plainer than by saying that Bilbo was *meant* to find the Ring, and not by its maker.[3]

There it is. As I have said from the start, outside forces were at work in Bilbo's life—forces all the way up to the Creator, Ilúvatar himself. Bilbo has a destiny and a purpose, and finding the Ruling Ring is a major component. As such, he is protected from the ring's dark influences because he already is in service to a greater Will, a more powerful Master.

As the apostle John says: "The one who is in you is greater than the one who is in the world" (1 John 4:4).

Deus Ex Machina

Are you familiar with the term *deus ex machina* (DAY-es ecks MACK-in-ah)? It's Latin for "god out of the machine," and it refers to those moments in stories when, in the face of a seemingly insurmountable obstacle, something completely unexpected suddenly emerges from the woodwork to change the circumstances or save the day.

The phrase probably originated as a reaction to Greek tragedies, which often called for characters playing gods to be lowered onto the stage, literally, using cranes. Within the plot, the erstwhile god (Hercules, for instance) used his divine powers to swing the action in a totally new direction.

As a literary technique, however, storytellers have been using *deus ex machina* for as long as there have been tales to tell. In *The Odyssey*, for example, Athena intervenes subtly on several occasions. But at the end she shows up right at the commencement of a final battle and commands everyone to stop and go home. (They obey.) In *Jurassic Park*, the film's protagonists are about to be cut down by velociraptors when, from out of nowhere, a Tyrannosaurus Rex attacks the raptors, allowing the humans to escape.

We even find biblical examples, such as the huge fish God "appoints" to swallow the prophet Jonah during a storm, for delivery to Nineveh.

Sometimes these surprises make sense and work well within the overall plot and pace of action. More often, though, a *deus ex machina* reveals an author's inability to come up with a satisfactory resolution to a problem or a plausible ending to the story.

Tolkien uses his own version of *deus ex machina* when the eagles rescue Gandalf, Bilbo, and the dwarves from the tops of burning trees.

Remember, Bilbo and his friends had an unfortunate encounter with wargs that forced them to scramble up those trees for safety. When goblins arrived and set the trees afire, their chances for escape went from poor to hopeless—until the eagles abruptly appeared to save the day.

Now, not all applications of this literary device are bad; this happens to be a "good" use of *deus ex machina*. The far-seeing eagles have eyries in the Misty Mountains—it makes sense within the realm of the story that they could see what was going on and would swoop down to frustrate the goblins.

Character Profile: The Eagles

In *The Silmarillion*'s creation accounts, Tolkien doesn't give many details on how the "normal" creatures of the world—mammals, reptiles, insects, etc.—were brought into being. But he does make clear connections between different members of the Valar and different areas of creation.

Ulmo, the Lord of Waters, governs the seas, lakes, rivers, and streams, as well as the creatures that live in those waters. Oromë, a mighty hunter, "delights in horses and hounds."[4] Yavanna, known as the Giver of Fruits, is "the lover of all things that grow in the earth."[5] And so on.

Manwë Súlimo is the most powerful member of the Valar. Early in *The Silmarillion* he is described as the being who "[is] dearest to Ilúvatar and understands most clearly his purposes."[6] He also is the Lord of Winds and, interestingly, he has a connection to several kinds of birds—especially eagles.

Indeed, he specifically sent them as watchers and guardians in the northern mountains.[7] So the eagles represent Manwë, who represents the will of Ilúvatar. Like Gandalf, they often act as Agents of Divine Rescue and Wrath.

We see this in *The Hobbit* when they pull Gandalf, the dwarves, and Bilbo from the trees and onward to safety. That's one example among many:

- In *The Hobbit*, the arrival of the eagles during The Battle of Five Armies ultimately turns the tide and allows the forces of good to defeat the goblins and other creatures of evil.

- In *The Fellowship of the Ring*, an eagle frees Gandalf from his bondage atop Saruman's tower.
- In *The Return of the King*, a host of eagles assists Aragorn and his forces at the Battle of Morannon. (Their entrance here parallels the earlier Battle of Five Armies.)
- In *The Return of the King*, several eagles carrying Gandalf rescue Frodo and Sam after the One Ring is destroyed.

Once again, there is a connection between Tolkien's use of eagles and how the birds are scripturally portrayed. Check out these verses:

This is what you are to say to the descendants of Jacob and what you are to tell the people of Israel: "You yourselves have seen what I did to Egypt, and how I carried you on eagles' wings and brought you to myself."

Exodus 19:3–4

Those who hope in the Lord
will renew their strength.
They will soar on wings like eagles;
they will run and not grow weary,
they will walk and not be faint.

Isaiah 40:31

Look! An eagle will soar and swoop down,
spreading its wings over Bozrah.
In that day the hearts of Edom's warriors
will be like the heart of a woman in labor.

Jeremiah 49:22

The woman was given the two wings of a great eagle, so that she might fly to the place prepared for her in the wilderness, where she would be taken care of for a time, times and half a time, out of the serpent's reach.

Revelation 12:14

What all this means is that the eagles are flying, breathing representations of *deus ex machina* throughout Tolkien's mythology—but not in any cheesy sense. Their presence in the stories demonstrates that Providence is watching; their actions show Providence willing and able to help in times of trouble.

7

A Blessed Rest

The Christian doctrine of the Sabbath is taken directly from Scripture:

> Remember the Sabbath day by keeping it holy. Six days you shall labor and do all your work, but the seventh day is a sabbath to the Lord your God. On it you shall not do any work, neither you, nor your son or daughter, nor your male or female servant, nor your animals, nor any foreigner residing in your towns. For in six days the Lord made the heavens and the earth, the sea, and all that is in them, but he rested on the seventh day.
>
> Exodus 20:8–11

The idea is as simple as it is practical: The God who made us intended our lives to be governed by regular patterns of work and rest—specifically, six days of the former followed by one day of the latter.

Houses of Rest

J. R. R. Tolkien followed a similar pattern with his characters during their adventures in *The Hobbit*. Yes, even in the wild lands beyond civilization's borders, the Sabbath holds sway. And that is the primary theme of chapter 7.

Actually, we've already seen one chapter at least partially dedicated to the theme of rest: chapter 3, where Thorin and Company took shelter in the House of Elrond. That chapter was also written with a keen eye toward the elves and their history (discussed earlier).

In the house of Beorn, however, rest and restoration take center stage. There, a brief stay allows Bilbo and his friends, who've just finished a harrowing confrontation with the goblins in the mountains, to recuperate. It also permits them to resupply and prepare themselves for the ominous, arduous journey through the evil forest of Mirkwood.

Again, this pattern—work and rest—continues throughout the story.

After many miserable weeks in Mirkwood, the group is given a reprieve in the halls of the wood elves (though it does come with prison bars). Then, surviving being half-killed in barrels after escaping incarceration, Bilbo and the dwarves are treated like kings by the men of Esgaroth, resupplied and refreshed before the end of their journey and the confrontation with Smaug.

Getting back to chapter 7, it's also interesting to note what Tolkien included (and excluded) in his ideal vision of rest. Beauty is a key element, for example. Beorn's house is surrounded by flowerbeds and green fields contrasting with rock and stone. It's an idyllic scene that perhaps even reflects the garden of Eden.

Food, excluding a certain type, also is a vital factor at Beorn's. There is bread and butter and honey and clotted cream, not to mention nuts, fruit, and pleasant drink. Beorn would not be considered a vegan by any stretch, but it's telling that nothing on his menu made death necessary to feed life.

Other facets of rest include telling stories, singing songs, smoking pipes, and, of course, sleeping snuggled up in blankets next to a fire, as Bilbo seems to do most often throughout this chapter.

Not found anywhere near Beorn's restful house are the machinations of industrialization. Everything is natural, from tables and chairs to servers and cooks. There are no instruments of gold or silver, no appliances or contraptions, no jarring noise.

All of this provides an intriguing window into Tolkien as a person, revealing his likes and dislikes through the window of story.

Literary Corner: Why Gandalf Had to Leave

One of the more distressing moments in the story, both for Bilbo and for us, comes when Gandalf takes his leave of the humble company. We are warned about his eventual departure at the beginning of chapter 7, but it still lands like a blow when the wizard rides away with the hobbit and the dwarves perched on the menacing doorstep of Mirkwood.

We readers have appreciated Gandalf's unique personality from the start, including his actions and his wit. It's clear to us that Bilbo and the dwarves would never have come this far without his help, and so we can't help but feel anxious for their safety as they prepare to move on without him.

Within the realm of Tolkien's larger mythology, we know Gandalf had to leave the company in order to join with the other wizards and drive Sauron (also called the Necromancer) out of his stronghold *in* Mirkwood. Gandalf says as much himself in *The Hobbit* chapter 19, and a few more details in the last section of *The Silmarillion* reveal that Sauron, anticipating this move, actually used the opportunity to sneak into his old fortresses in Mordor.

Still, we wonder: How can Thorin and Company possibly make it alone?

In reality, that's rather the point—they *need* to make it on their own. Or, more specifically, *Bilbo* needs to make it on *his* own.

The hobbit was intended to be, is destined to become, a hero. But he has limited opportunity to become what he was created to be as long as Gandalf is around to fix problems and get everyone out of sticky situations. Gandalf left to make room for Bilbo's growth—for Bilbo to become a "new creation."

What is more, Tolkien is following centuries of literary tradition by moving Gandalf out of the way and allowing Bilbo to flourish.

Many authors use old, wise, and powerful characters as mentors for budding heroes or heroines. At some point, however, the mentor must be removed so that his or her charge can actualize potential.

The relationship between Merlin and King Arthur was an early example of this phenomenon. A more recent example would be Albus Dumbledore and Harry Potter, and there have been many more in between, including Gandalf.

This is the point: Bilbo can only earn his stripes by overcoming adversity on his own in order to become what he was created to be.

8

A New Hobbit

sing the megaphone of his mythology, J. R. R. Tolkien had a lot to say about good and evil. But he often chose different ways to speak about these topics.

For example, he typically expressed things good and honorable in a subtle manner. Oftentimes they are hidden until needed, as with Bilbo's courage and Aragorn's nobility. Other times the most powerful virtues are displayed in seemingly small acts, such as Bilbo refusing to attack an unarmed Gollum and instead allowing himself to feel compassion.

When Tolkien writes about evil, however, it's a different approach. The presence of wickedness is almost always announced through bigness and brash actions and clamorous noise. The trolls are huge and menacing. The goblins always appear in yammering hordes. Mordor is always described in connection with billowing smoke and reeking vapors.

All these principles can be found in *The Hobbit*, to one degree or another. But this contrast between good and evil stands out sharply in chapter 8.

Oppressive Evil

We know from Beorn's (and Gandalf's) descriptions that Mirkwood is a place of malevolence. Yet that wasn't always the case. *The Silmarillion* says it once was called Greenwood the Great, and it represented nature at its finest. Until Sauron came to live there.

As Bilbo and the dwarves journey through this forest, they meet evil's presence in a variety of ways. First and most obvious is the absence of light.

Remember that in Middle-earth, the sun, moon, and stars had been set in the sky by the angelic Valar. The light they produce is both a challenge to evil and a reminder of Ilúvatar's divine presence and guidance in the world.

That's why it's worthy of note that Bilbo and his friends are not oppressed by the presence of nighttime in Mirkwood. It's not really the darkness that bothers them. Rather, what presses down on them and chokes them and drives them crazy is the absence of any kind of light. Tolkien describes their misery in terms of suffocation—without light, they feel squeezed out of something vital to being.

This contrast between light and darkness serves as another link and reflection between Tolkien's world and Scripture. Bilbo's plight, for instance, echoes the words of Job:

> Have I not wept for those in trouble?
> Has not my soul grieved for the poor?

Yet when I hoped for good, evil came;
when I looked for light, then came darkness.
The churning inside me never stops;
days of suffering confront me.
I go about blackened, but not by the sun;
I stand up in the assembly and cry for help.

Job 30:25–28

Again, Jesus used this contrast to describe the Incarnation (and our sinful response to it): "This is the verdict: Light has come into the world, but people loved darkness instead of light because their deeds were evil" (John 3:19).

Another way Bilbo and the dwarves experience evil's nearness is through the twisting of what should have been good. They find squirrels and other animals that would normally serve as food, for example, but in Mirkwood, everything—even the plants—is inedible. It's all corrupted.

They are also desperate for water, but the only stream they come across is black with enchantment; it causes Bombur to fall into an un-wakeable sleep. What should have provided nourishment instead heaps on to their burdens.

Bilbo and the dwarves also endure the presence of malevolence in massive and ravenous spiders—but I'll get to that in a minute.

A Second Failure

For now, a question to consider: Does the plight of Bilbo and the dwarves in Mirkwood seem familiar at all? Because it should.

Think all the way back to chapter 2, when Gandalf had briefly left the company in order to scout the road ahead. Bilbo and the dwarves, hungry and grumpy, happened to spot a fire burning in the distance. The hobbit, sent to investigate, sparked a chain of events through which all the dwarves were tied up in sacks and had to be rescued by the wizard.

Back to chapter 8: Gandalf is gone again. The group is again grumpy and hungry—*starving* might be a better description. And wouldn't you know it, they see another fire in the distance.

What will they do? Surely they learned from mistakes during the earlier incident, right? Surely they won't make the same error twice, especially since Gandalf *and* Beorn expressly told everyone not to leave the path.

Alas, they succumb to temptation once more and depart the way in order to find out the source of the fire. In so doing, they resemble the people Paul describes in Philippians 3:19: "Their destiny is destruction, their god is their stomach, and their glory is in their shame. Their mind is set on earthly things."

What's most discouraging about this whole incident is that Bilbo fails to do his job as Gandalf's replacement— just as he failed to do right with the trolls. Indeed, along with Bombur, Bilbo is the leader of those arguing to ignore Gandalf's instructions and leave the path in search of food. Again he has drifted back to his "old self."

What's the result? Instead of being stuffed in sacks, this time the dwarves are cocooned in webs, poisoned, and hung from a tree. Truly the results of this failure are dire.

Fortunately for them, later in the chapter Bilbo does much better on his second test of leadership.

A Time to Sting

At his nadir in Mirkwood, Bilbo finds himself alone in the blackness, half-cocooned in silk, and facing an agitated giant spider. Talk about a classic "horrible, no good, very bad day."

This is another watershed moment for Bilbo and his development as the hero of his own story. He has been taking strides and showing growth through recent adventures. He yelled to alert Gandalf when goblins confronted him in the cave. He pressed forward in the tunnels when he was alone and terrified. He matched wits with Gollum and then successfully escaped the orcs.

But now, staring at eight gleaming eyes and eight hairy legs, something new is required. There is no escape this time. Bilbo must stand and fight.

And he does. Remembering his little sword, he fights. And against all hope—miracle of miracles—he wins. Look how far he has come! The hobbit who dreamed of one day *carrying* a sword has now brandished his blade in a fight to the death. The hobbit who sought to earn praise from his friends by pilfering from a pocket has now slain a monstrous creature for the prize of life—his and the lives of his friends.

This is a momentous occasion, and once the initial shock wears off, Bilbo grasps the significance of what he has done. He feels like a different person.

What's fascinating to note is that such growth occurred directly because of Bilbo's experiences with suffering and tribulations. In many ways he has become a walking example of what the apostle Peter wrote concerning strength and endurance in the face of affliction and evil:

> Be alert and of sober mind. Your enemy the devil prowls around like a roaring lion looking for someone to devour. Resist him, standing firm in the faith, because you know that the family of believers throughout the world is undergoing the same kind of sufferings.

And the God of all grace, who called you to his eternal glory in Christ, after you have suffered a little while, will himself restore you and make you strong, firm and steadfast.

1 Peter 5:8–10

Here's what I'm saying: The trolls, the goblins, the Gollum encounter, the long miles with little food or decent rest—all these have combined to sharpen the hobbit and hone him into something new and better: a weapon.

Yes, just like Gandalf, Bilbo has now taken his place as an Agent of Divine Wrath. He has confronted evil and destroyed it.

Nevertheless, the little hobbit isn't done yet. He has another leap to make in this very chapter, one that involves his friends—plus a lot more spiders.

A Time to Save

Imagine you are Bilbo Baggins, travelling through a dark forest in search of your missing friends. You come across a patch of darkness that is somehow more substantial than the "regular" darkness around you—something "black like a patch of midnight"[1] that refused to be banished by the light of the sun.

As you near it, you ascertain that the blackness is caused by gargantuan webs strung all around a large clearing. Getting closer still, you realize the webs are populated by enormous spiders—many, *many* enormous spiders.

If you found yourself in that spot, what would you do? I think I'd flee as fast as my legs could move!

That's not what Bilbo does, of course. He has been altered by recent events, and already he is a very different hobbit from the one who entered Mirkwood—let alone the one who ran out of his house back in the Shire without any pocket-handkerchiefs.

I want to make three observations about this arachnid encounter.

First, we need to understand that newfound courage doesn't eliminate fear. Bilbo still feels afraid of the spiders (as he should). He still trembles, still wants to remain unseen. What has changed, essentially, is how Bilbo deals with his fear: He no longer allows it to control him, no longer prizes his comfort and security so highly that fear's presence compels him to seek safety above any other concern.

How do we know this? Because despite his fear—despite his desire to remain unnoticed—he intentionally arouses the monsters' anger and *entices them to chase after him*! More, he attacks them when necessary.

That leads to my second observation: Bilbo's actions with the spiders fortify his status as an Agent of Divine Wrath. Simply put, little Bilbo has become an awesome force in the war against evil.

As the strength of the dwarves begins to flag, Bilbo appears out of nowhere and charges into the astonished spiders. He darts back and forth, slashing at webs and spider-legs with his little sword—even stabbing the spiders' fat bodies if they come to near. This enrages the spiders to the point of cursing their little enemy, but they don't dare come near him because they're mortally afraid of Sting.

It's astonishing to see the metamorphosis of Bilbo Baggins. The hobbit who swelled with pride after his recent leap to killing one spider now takes on a multitude in their own colony. No longer racing from danger, he attacks. As a result, the beasts mortally fear *him*!

Now, the third observation: Bilbo's actions with the spiders cement his standing as an Agent of Divine Rescue.

I've mentioned that many Mirkwood events have a connection to the company's interaction with the trolls in chapter 2. Then, Gandalf was the Agent. He discovered the dwarves in mortal danger—stuck in sacks, one step away from growling troll bellies—and Bilbo nowhere in sight.

In Mirkwood, it's Bilbo who finds the dwarves in such peril—wrapped in spider webs and one step from a fatal poisoning—and Gandalf is far away. Like the wizard, Bilbo spins a cunning plan to lure the spiders from the dwarves. But his actions go a step further as he puts his own life in danger to effect their rescue. He uses himself as bait to attract attention, then later he physically fights off the spiders to give the dwarves opportunity for escape.

This transcends courage and bravery and heroic action. This demonstration of self-sacrificial love reflects the words of Jesus: "Greater love has no one than this: to lay down one's life for one's friends" (John 15:13).

Like Gandalf before him, the hobbit now actively works to achieve the will of Providence not only by destroying evil but also by offering salvation and rescue to those in need.

9

The Hidden Hero

Thus far in the story, Bilbo's time in Mirkwood has been nothing less than transformational. And in many ways, his experiences actually have served as microcosms of the major themes I've been highlighting throughout this book.

For example, his most significant growth develops amid his most significant trials (James 1:2–4). On a divine mission, he destroys whatever forces of evil attempt to stand in his way (Psalm 92:7). He puts his life on the line in order to rescue his friends (Galatians 1:3). And the weakest player in the forest ends up shaming the creatures who had considered themselves strong (1 Corinthians 1:26–29).

In chapter 8, Bilbo replaced Gandalf within the company as Agents of Divine Wrath and Rescue. Now he will take on yet another mantle as Agent of Divine Initiation—and herein officially will become the expedition's leader.

Bilbo for President

Actually, Bilbo's ascension into leadership started back before the dwarves were captured by the wood elves.

At chapter 8's beginning, after Gandalf's departure, we don't get a clear sense of who's leading the company. At moments it seems Bilbo is already in command, such as when he takes charge of snagging the boat across the enchanted stream. But in other moments Thorin gives out orders, as when he directs Bilbo to climb a tree and note their progress through the forest.

After battling the spiders, the dwarves all turn to Bilbo when they realize Thorin is gone. Indeed, they not only look to him for a plan of escape, they go so far as to pledge themselves to his service and bow in front of him!

Still, we wonder, what will happen once Thorin rejoins the company?

That question, and that of leadership in general, is resolved once and for all in chapter 9. Held captive, unsure of his friends' fate, Thorin becomes despondent. He loses hope to where he considers telling the Elvenking all about the treasure and his quest—a desperate maneuver for a dwarf, certainly.

That's when Bilbo finds the king of the dwarves and restores his faith. From that point on, Thorin and the other dwarves willingly rest in their cells and wait for Mr. Baggins to come up with a plan. They trust the hobbit entirely— which is what Gandalf said would happen.

In other words, the torch of leadership has been passed.

At first, though, it's not a happy development for Bilbo. Killing spiders in the heat of battle is one thing, but carrying the responsibility of his friends' well-being? Forming strategies for the success of the quest? Figuring out how to escape? These new task-types place a heavy burden on hobbit shoulders.

Even so, as with everything else now, Bilbo rises to the occasion. He takes ownership. He makes the necessary plans. And he helps the entire company escape, thus preserving their venture.

Bilbo even rises to deft handling of dissension in the ranks. When the dwarves learn of his design to escape the cave in barrels, they grumble and complain. They call him crazy, alleging he should have thought of something more sensible.

Nonplussed, he rebuffs the arguments with a bit of Gandalf-ish sternness. He offers to take them back to their nice cells and let them sit there comfortably until they think of a better plan—although he reminds them he probably won't be able to get the keys again, even if he felt inclined to try.

To see how the hobbit has grown, we need only compare this speech with the quivering, spluttering, self-justifying creature hosting the unexpected party in chapter 1. Truly, the old Bilbo is gone, and the new Bilbo is being formed.

Now he is an Agent of Divine Wrath, and of Rescue, and, like Gandalf, of Initiation. He is a hero, he is a leader, and he will be in need all of his pristine skills through the journey still ahead.

Naturally, he also will need a spot of luck.

Fortune and Providence

That's a key word to keep an eye out for in chapter 9: *luck*. The narrator repeats it several times when describing Bilbo's various efforts in the wood elves' cave, and he'll continue to use it through the hobbit's remaining adventures.

Today, the idea of luck is often associated with negative implications. "He only won because he was lucky," for example, or, "She's done all she can; the outcome will just have to come down to luck." In the contemporary sense, *luck* often implies a lack of skill or competence.

In Tolkien's mythology, however, *luck* carries a different weight—the weight of divinity.

Proverbs 16:33 says: "The lot is cast into the lap, but its every decision is from the Lord." This theme appears often throughout Scripture, especially in the Old Testament. All kinds of people cast lots to make decisions—from kings to priests to peasants. And yet such actions did not imply that random chance decided what would happen. Rather, that worldview placed even something like rolling dice under the direct authority of God.

Thus, what we refer to as "luck," they would have seen as divine action. What we refer to as "random chance," they would have seen as Providence.

The latter view is very much in operation throughout *The Hobbit* as well as Tolkien's legendarium on the whole. Several actions and events are credited to luck or good fortune—lots of rescues and escapes that come "just in the nick of time."

A few examples in chapter 9:

- The wood elves capture Bilbo and the dwarves when they're on the brink of starvation.
- Bilbo happens to hear a guard talking about a thirteenth dwarf held deep in the cave, which turns out to be Thorin.
- When Bilbo overhears the butler talking of clearing out the empty barrels later in the evening, he realizes that "luck was with him."[1]
- The butler and the chief of the guards being rendered unconscious by Dorwinion's wine is ascribed to "luck of an unusual kind."[2]
- Bilbo finishes packing the dwarves in barrels just a minute before the elves come in to send them down the river.

- While Bilbo is initially forced to splutter in the river, his "luck turned"[3] quickly when the rafts became stuck on a hidden root, allowing him to scramble out of the water.

That's a lot of good fortune! In the hands of another author, all these expressions might seem like overindulgence of a theme or even poor writing.

For Tolkien, however, such examples are meant to reflect the ever-present, ever-helping hand of Providence.

Subtle Compassion

Before we move on, there's a quick cave incident to highlight and explore.

After Bilbo sees the butler and the chief guard succumb to their wine, he takes the keys from the guard in order to free his friends. The whole affair is a lucky stroke, and Bilbo takes advantage of the situation in an admirable way.

But what happens as Bilbo and the dwarves pass them—both still asleep on the table—en route to freedom? Stealthily, silently, the hobbit sneaks back into the room and reattaches the guard's keys. The returned keys will save the guard some trouble, Bilbo notes, remembering that the guard wasn't a bad fellow and treated the prisoners well.

Do not overlook this incident. It happens quickly. It is subtle and has little meaning within the overall chapter, yet I believe it to be a vitally central moment, for two reasons.

First, it shows that, even with all the transformations he has experienced within Mirkwood, Bilbo has retained his capacity for thoughtful kindness and good-natured compassion. He has not gained courage only to lose empathy. He is compounding, not replacing, his virtues.

This is no small matter. As Bilbo has recently become leader of his small troop, it would be easy for him to adopt an "us versus the world" mentality. It would be easy for him to view anyone standing between him and his goals as an enemy. Easy, but destructive—to the hobbit and to his overall mission.

No, Bilbo realizes he is part of the forces of good. His enemies are the forces of evil, not two elves incidentally caught up in a misunderstanding. As Jesus said: "Whoever is not against you is for you" (Luke 9:50).

This wisdom will serve the hobbit well when he must make difficult choices after the destruction of Smaug (and before the Battle of Five Armies).

Second, this moment is important because of the Ruling Ring. Bilbo has been forced to stay invisible within the wood elves' caves, which means he's been wearing it nonstop for several weeks. And since he has no idea about the ring's actual history, he has no awareness of what kind of danger he's in.

But we do. We know the ring is deadly, a vehicle of destruction and carnage. And we worry that Bilbo's prolonged exposure will wreak havoc.

That's why we should be relieved to see him perform this simple act of kindness. Bilbo's ability to behave decently—kindheartedly—toward the chief guard shows that the ring's influence over the hobbit remains minor. Indeed, it's probable that his kindnesses are what prevent the ring from gaining a stronger foothold.

These little moments of gentle virtue are why, decades later, Bilbo is able to pass the ring over to Frodo and move on down the road, unharmed.

10

The Long-Awaited Party

The old saying that "no good deed goes unpunished" holds true here, at least, for this is what Bilbo experiences after freeing his friends from their barrels after a long ride down the river.

At first the bedraggled dwarves are very ornery *and* very ungrateful.

Gradually, however, they begin to appreciate their freedom, and—grudgingly—they offer Bilbo a few meager words of thanks.

The company's next step is a trip into Lake-town. The next step for us, perhaps surprisingly, is a discussion on the nature and role of prophecy—in Tolkien's world and in Scripture.

Old Songs

The Bible is full of prophecies. Whether Old Testament or New, epistles or histories, minor prophets or major—its pages are packed with proclamations about future events. The *Encyclopedia of Biblical Prophecy* claims to document 1,817 biblical prophecies.[1]

Despite such frequency, many believers remain confused about prophecy's role in Scripture. Those who do take a stand on biblical prophecy regularly tend toward one of two extremes.

Some Christians take an approach that's almost disdainful. They find prophecy unhelpful, sometimes even embarrassing. These people view biblical prophecy as a relic from the ancient cultures in which the Scriptures were written. While these may have impacted people a long time ago, they don't have much application in a "modern" world.

At the spectrum's other end are Christians who exalt prophecy and emphasize it highly. These people believe prophecies are indeed viable in today's world. Even more, they maintain that prophecies can be studied, interpreted, and ultimately used to accurately predict future happenings.

As is often the case, the middle ground between these two extremes offers a more helpful (and more accurate) understanding of biblical prophecy.

On one hand, scriptural prophecies should be considered true and applicable because the entire Bible is true and applicable (2 Timothy 3:16). Prophetic words were inspired by the Holy Spirit for a specific purpose, and whatever that purpose is, it should not be ignored.

On the other hand, the purpose of biblical prophecy has almost nothing to do with forecasting the future. Such prophecies usually contain several layers of meaning, which makes it impossible to dissect them as a way of making anything but the vaguest predictions about what lies ahead.

Here is an example I included in *The Bible Answer Book*:

> Consider Isaiah's prophecy of Jesus being born of a virgin: "Therefore the Lord himself will give you a sign: The virgin will be with child and will give birth to a son, and will call him Immanuel. He will eat curds and honey when he knows enough to reject the wrong and choose the right. But before the boy knows enough to reject the wrong and choose the right, the land of the two kings you dread will be laid waste" (7:14).
>
> This prophecy applies to two periods of time. The phrase "two kings you dread" refers to Rezin and Pekah, who were kings of Aram and Israel, respectively, enemies that were threatening to attack Judah. On one level, the prophecy is saying that in only a short time, the people of Judah would have no reason to fear those nations, and indeed, they were conquered by the Assyrians. On a second level, however, the prophecy also points to the Messiah, born of a virgin, as a sign that God would not abandon his people.[2]

Biblical prophecy is meant to help readers look backward as well as forward. As we look through the Scriptures and observe the many prophecies that already have been fulfilled historically, our faith increases.

The prophecies in Tolkien's world follow a similar principle.

Old Songs in Middle-Earth

In *The Hobbit*, chapter 10 is the first time we run across the idea of prophecy. Before Bilbo begins to unpack the dwarves from their barrels, we learn that the older men of Lake-town sometimes sang songs about the return of

Thrain or Thrór (Thorin's father and grandfather), which would cause gold to flow in the rivers and bring new songs and laughter into the land.

That is a relatively minor prophetic matter, and we're assured the people viewed the legend as pleasant without allowing it to affect their daily business.

And yet it does produce an impact when Thorin proclaims himself King under the Mountain who has returned to claim his own. His declaration would produce two kinds of reactions.

First, the majority of the people in Lake-town felt a kind of exuberant expectation. Some of the guards ran outside to look at the water, for example, as if they expected to see the rivers turn golden right under their feet. Others in the crowd instantly bestowed celebrity status on the dwarves, and for more than a week the entire town was filled with songs of the dragon's defeat and of gold flowing down the mountain to meet their needs.

These reactions are not positive, however, and Tolkien presents them as unwise, even childish—especially since Smaug is still alive and menacing in the bowels of the mountain.

The second reaction-type was fear. Seeing Thorin's kingly demeanor, the wood elves who steered the barrel-raft began to wonder if their king had made a mistake; they're afraid. Later, when Thorin approaches the town's master about supplies for an expedition to the Lonely Mountain, at first the master is surprised—he thought the dwarves were imposters and never expected them to actually approach the dragon. Then he too becomes afraid.

While the crowd's exuberance was a sign of foolishness, the presence of fear was a sign of wisdom—or at least of perception. The wood elves and the master had begun to realize that something larger than normal was occurring.

Extraordinary forces were at work; something big was about to happen.

In Tolkien's world, that's a proper reaction to the concept of prophecy.

Interestingly, once the dwarves leave town and make their trek toward the mountain, all talk of prophecy ceases. The old songs don't influence what actually happens between the dragon and Thorin's Company, nor do they play a part in the Battle of Five Armies.

In fact, the only other time we hear about the prophecies is on the book's very last page, when Balin reports on the prosperity of the rebuilt Lake-town and the new songs that sing of gold flowing down the mountain. Bilbo exclaims that the old songs have turned out to be true, "after a fashion."

Gandalf wants to know why they shouldn't prove true. He says Bilbo shouldn't disbelieve the prophecies simply because he had a hand in bringing them about—and he reminds the hobbit that all of his escapes weren't managed by sheer luck alone, nor did they come about solely for his benefit.

This is the crux of the matter.

Like the God of the Bible, Ilúvatar has full knowledge of both past and future. Before prophecies are fulfilled, they serve to remind of His knowledge. After they are fulfilled, they serve to remind of His guidance and care.

That is, prophecies are important because they point to Providence.

Character Profile: The Dwarves

Since we're talking about old songs and kings under the mountain, this is a great time to explore the history of the dwarves and their collective role within *The Hobbit*.

THE HISTORY OF THE DWARVES

Here's a fascinating tidbit of information: According to *The Silmarillion*, the dwarves were the first sentient beings (other than the Valar) to awaken in Middle-earth. That wasn't supposed to be the case, however.

When the Valar entered the world, Ilúvatar instructed them to shape it in preparation for the arrival of elves and men—elves being the "firstborn," and men coming after. The preparation included setting boundaries around the sea, carving out mountains, giving life to trees/other vegetation, and a lot more.

When all of this was finished, some of the Valar became restless as they waited for the firstborn to arrive. One of these was the earlier-mentioned Aulë.

Aulë took pleasure in mining, smithcraft, and the making of gems. But he also had a secret desire: He wanted to create conscious beings like himself—a race of people to whom he could teach all of his arts and whom he might guide in the making of beautiful things. Thus, he secretly made the dwarves.

Of course the secret was not hidden from Ilúvatar, though, and he confronted Aulë as soon as life entered the bodies of the dwarves. Ilúvatar didn't scold Aulë; rather, he pointed out that the dwarves possessed no minds of their own. Their thoughts were chained entirely to Aulë's will, because Ilúvatar alone can create a sentient being.

Aulë was shocked by this realization. He'd wanted to create something "other"—something he could interact with and teach and love. Instead, he had produced mindless automatons who could not resist his will.

Despairing, Aulë picked up a hammer to destroy his creations, but Ilúvatar told him not to strike. Compassionately, Ilúvatar unchained the minds of the dwarves and granted them sentient thought. Even so, he would not allow them to populate the earth before the elves, and thus he put them into a deep sleep until after the firstborn had come.

Amid these events, Ilúvatar makes an interesting comment to Aulë:

> Even as I gave being to the thoughts of the Ainur at the beginning of the World, so now I have taken up thy desire and given to it a place therein; but in no other way will I amend thy handiwork, and as thou hast made it, so shall it be.[3]

Not exactly a ringing endorsement! It's almost as if Ilúvatar were saying "Be careful what you wish for."

And indeed, the dwarves' history in Middle-earth is full of ups and downs. At times they act bravely and fight against Melkor and the forces of evil with grim ferocity. Other times they appear disinterested in anything happening outside their own halls and businesses—some dwarves, driven by greed, even join forces with goblins and other creatures of evil.

Like Aulë, the dwarves demonstrate tremendous skill at mining, forging, and crafting. Many times they use those skills to produce works of profound value and beauty that bless other inhabitants of the land. Other times, though, they are driven to wicked deeds by lust and greed—both for objects of their own craftsmanship and the material achievements of others.

One of the most intriguing dynamics regarding the dwarves' history is their complex relationship with the elves of Middle-earth. In the world's earlier ages, dwarves held a strong allegiance with elves—especially with the Noldor who came from Valinor. Those elves shared the dwarves' love of mining and craftsmanship and were willing to teach the dwarves techniques they had learned from the Valar.

However, one particular incident caused a major rift between the races.

Thingol the elf, king of a realm called Doriath, came into possession of a Silmaril—one of the loveliest and most valuable jewels in the world—through the efforts of Beren and Lúthien (Elrond's ancestors). Thingol commissioned several dwarves to set the jewel in a magnificent necklace, and the end result was more captivating than anything previously seen in Middle-earth.

It was so captivating, in fact, that the group of dwarves who had worked on it slew Thingol and with it fled back to their home. They in turn were slain, and these episodes sparked both a full-out war between the two kingdoms and a simmering enmity between elves and dwarves ever after.

Perhaps the best—and most damning—summary of the dwarves is found in *The Hobbit* chapter 12, before Bilbo first goes into Smaug's tunnel. The narrator tells us that dwarves are not, by nature, heroic. Some are "pretty bad lots," whereas most are "decent enough . . . if you don't expect too much"[4]

Again, this is no ringing endorsement by any means—but it's a true statement, as we will see in later chapters.

Here are a few more useful facts about dwarves before we move on to their role in *The Hobbit*:

- Dwarves stand between half and three-quarters as tall as an average man, although they are much broader and stockier.
- Dwarves can live several hundred years. (In Mirkwood, Thorin says his eyes don't work as well as they did a hundred years ago.)
- Dwarves have tremendous endurance and stamina when it comes to physical activity. They can run

for miles and miles at a time even while wearing heavy armor and carrying supplies.

• Dúrin, whom Thorin mentions several times as his ancestor, was one of the seven original dwarf fathers created by Aulë.

THE DWARVES' ROLE IN THIS SEGMENT OF THE STORY

Obviously, Thorin and Company play a vital role in advancing the plot of Bilbo's adventures. Their quest to reach the Lonely Mountain, deal with Smaug, and recover their treasure is what enables Gandalf to recruit Bilbo in the first place. And, presumably, it's Thorin who finances the entire operation.

In addition, the dwarves add much depth and diversity to the story through their different personalities and attributes. Bombur regularly provides an element of comic relief. Thorin adds a touch of seriousness, even darkness at times. Old Balin brings kindness and compassion (for a dwarf). And so on.

The dwarves' main function in *The Hobbit*, though, has little to do with the action or with creative devices. Thorin and his companions serve as an excellent foil for Bilbo, which helps us monitor the hobbit's growth from chapter to chapter.

The reason the dwarves provide such a valuable point of comparison is that they don't change throughout the story. That they remain constant in their attitudes, opinions, and characteristics makes them an ideal control (a placebo, of sorts) in connection with Mr. Baggins.

In the early stages of the journey, the dwarves make it obvious that Bilbo is entirely out of place when it comes to adventures. Their preparation highlights his lack thereof (and his lack of pocket-handkerchiefs). Their familiarity with the geography of the land magnifies Bilbo's ignorance. And their occasional bravery—think of Thorin grabbing a flaming stick to fight the trolls—spotlights Bilbo's cowardice in the face of fear.

As the story progresses, however, the gap begins to narrow. The company's dependence on Gandalf showcases those times when Bilbo is forced to figure out solutions on his own, such as his battle of wits with Gollum in the roots of the mountain. And their character flaws—all the way from surliness to fury—help us see the various ways in which Bilbo has experienced personal growth.

By the end, everything is inverted. The dwarves haven't changed at all—they're still a collection of decent yet worldly fellows who've charged into an adventure that's over their heads. When we see them side-by-side with Bilbo, however, the hobbit shines.

For one thing, at several points Bilbo demonstrates genuine courage up against real danger—most notably his willingness to walk down a dark tunnel and confront a dragon. In light of this hard-won heroism, the dwarves' bravery looks much more like periodic bursts of self-preservation.

Even more, the hobbit's generosity and willingness to sacrifice for the sake of others casts a spotlight on the dwarves' pervasive stubbornness, calculating nature, and outright greed. This will be especially apparent as we explore the final chapters of Bilbo's story.

11

The Waiting
Is the Hardest Part

Quick survey: Do you like it when a restaurant hostess hands you a flashing buzzer and says, "It'll be about forty minutes"? When you sit down in the little room outside your doctor's office and pick up a magazine dated eight months ago, do you feel cheerful about what will happen next? By and large, do you have positive inclinations toward traffic jams?

I'm willing to guess you answered no to all three questions.

Most people hate waiting. It's another universal experience none of us can avoid no matter how hard we try. And it gets no easier with practice. In fact, the more we are forced to wait, the more loathsome waiting seems.

According to chapter 11 of Bilbo's journey, these human sentiments are shared among hobbits and dwarves as well.

Inverted Triumph

It has been a long journey for Fili, Kili, Oin, Gloin, Dwalin, Balin, Bifur, Bofur, Bombur, Dori, Nori, Ori, Thorin, and Bilbo. The company that first came together all the way back in the Shire has passed through many lands and survived many dangers.

They've ridden through the Lone-lands and brawled with trolls. They've been refreshed in Rivendell. They've climbed the wearying paths of the Misty Mountains, sprinted through the terrifying tunnels underneath, and warred with orcs and wargs. They've perched on the eyries of eagles and even traversed on the backs of those majestic birds. They've been rejuvenated in the house of Beorn. They've trudged through lightless, airless Mirkwood. They've clashed with spiders. They've been imprisoned by elves and escaped, only to arrive half-alive at Esgaroth and the Long Lake.

And now, after fighting tooth and nail for every grim step and exhausting advance, Thorin and Company pass the final stretch and make camp at the base of the Lonely Mountain. The outbound jaunt is over. They have arrived.

We who have anticipated this event for more than two-thirds of the story might well expect a moment of triumph and exaltation from our protagonists. But such emotions are missing entirely from this part of the narrative.

Awaiting celebration, we're told explicitly that, rather, there is no "song or sound of harps."[1] Expecting joy and mirth, we learn there is "no laughter."[2] Thinking we'll sense a collective satisfaction at what they've accomplished, what they've overcome, and what they expect to reclaim, we find instead that the dwarves have become resigned to a "plodding gloom."[3]

There are two main reasons for such dejection at this juncture. The first and most obvious is the dragon. Bilbo and the dwarves see steam and dark smoke pouring from the front gate under the mountain—all but guaranteeing both the reality of Smaug and his nearness somewhere within those bowels.

All along the way, the dwarves in particular (not so much Bilbo) had envisioned Smaug as a goal to be reached. Now that they've reached him, he suddenly has transmogrified into a problem that must be solved. And what a big problem he is, at that.

The second reason for their lack of spirit: The waiting is compounded with boredom. Upon first arriving, Bilbo and the dwarves spent several days wandering along the mountain's surface on its western edge, seeking the hidden door indicated on Thorin's map. The dullness of their search would have been broken only if Smaug had burst into the air and been upon them.

When Bilbo does finally find a path leading up to the back door, the general mood improves for an evening. However, the dwarves then prove unable to open the door through cleverness, through spells, even through force. Things get so desperate that they bang on it with picks and hammers, despite the dragon's presence! Despair once more settles over the camp.

For months and months Bilbo and friends have been on the offensive. Actively, and among other things, they've been riding, running, climbing, singing, laughing, hiding, and floating. Now they're forced to sit. And wait. And stare at a locked door with no clue about how to get to its other side.

Autobiographical Waiting

For Tolkien, this time of frustrated waiting pointed back to his experiences during World War I—or the Great War, as it was known by his generation.

A signals officer, he spent more than a year as part of the Thirteenth and Eleventh Battalions of the Lancashire Fusiliers. He trained for months in several locations and saw live action at the Battle of the Somme. In October 1916, though, he was diagnosed with trench fever and taken out of service. He spent several more months in military hospitals before returning to England and pursuing his academic (and writing) career.

Tolkien later characterized his time in the army in these terms: long periods of waiting interspersed with bursts of chaotic action. He dealt with inclement weather, oozing mud, freezing temperatures, and the constant lethal threats of enemy soldiers and their shells.

Nevertheless, he frequently was bored out of his mind. Communicating with a friend during the war, he wrote:

> These grey days wasted in wearily going over, over and over again, the dreary topics, the dull backwaters of the art of killing, are not enjoyable.[4]

In another letter he added this description of what he found to be typical:

> The usual kind of morning standing about freezing and then trotting to get warmer so as to freeze again. We ended up by an hour's bomb-throwing with dummies. Lunch and a freezing afternoon . . . we stand in icy groups in the open being talked at! Tea and another scramble—I fought for a place at the stove and made a piece of toast on the end of a knife: what days![5]

Most certainly was he able to empathize with the frustration of Bilbo and the dwarves, then, as they milled about aimlessly on a spur of the mountain.

Biblical Waiting

Scripture contains several examples of people who, having received a call to take a certain action or a promise to receive a certain gift, were required to wait long periods of time before the fulfillment of that call or promise. In fact, the phenomenon is sufficiently common to have spawned the phrase "waiting on the Lord" for entry into our unofficial Christian lexicon.

Of all the biblical men and women who experienced this waiting, the story of Abraham is the most striking. He was still known as "Abram" at the time when he is introduced:

> The Lord had said to Abram, "Go from your country, your people and your father's household to the land I will show you.
>
> I will make you into a great nation,
> and I will bless you;
> I will make your name great,
> and you will be a blessing.
> I will bless those who bless you,
> and whoever curses you I will curse;
> and all peoples on earth
> will be blessed through you."
>
> So Abram went, as the Lord had told him; and Lot [his nephew] went with him. Abram was seventy-five years old when he set out from Harran.
>
> Genesis 12:1–4

God's words shocked Abraham from three directions:
(1) He had no children; (2) he was already seventy-five;
and (3) his wife, Sarah, was sixty-five, had been barren
her entire life, and had already experienced menopause.

By any practical standard of judgment, it was unwork-
able for Abraham and Sarah to produce a child—and thus,
by the same measure, it was not possible for him to become a "great nation" and somehow provide blessing to
"all peoples." Nonetheless, the Scriptures emphasize that
Abraham believed what God had said. Like Bilbo Baggins,
he accepted the call to an apparently impossible quest for
what was a seemingly unattainable result.

Here's what happens a little later:

> When Abram was ninety-nine years old, the Lord appeared
> to him and said, "I am God Almighty; walk before me faith-
> fully and be blameless. Then I will make my covenant be-
> tween me and you and will greatly increase your numbers."
>
> Abram fell facedown, and God said to him, "As for
> me, this is my covenant with you: You will be the father of
> many nations. No longer will you be called Abram; your
> name will be Abraham, for I have made you a father of
> many nations. I will make you very fruitful; I will make
> nations of you, and kings will come from you."
>
> Genesis 17:1–6

Did you catch that? He was seventy-five when he first
received God's promise of a coming son. And then, twenty-
four years later, God changed his name from Abram (which
means "exalted father") to Abraham (which means "father
of many"). This alteration may have been a bit hard to
swallow, seeing as nearly a quarter century later *he still
hadn't received the promised child!*

In fact, Isaac wasn't born until another full year had
passed. Abraham was a hundred years old when he finally

received his son—a full twenty-five years after God guaranteed it would happen.

Again, plenty of biblical others also experienced this "waiting on the Lord." After leaving Egypt, the Israelites wandered in the wilderness forty years before finally entering the Promised Land (Numbers 32:13).

David waited approximately fifteen years from when he was anointed as Israel's next king until he actually ascended to the throne in Hebron. And then he waited another seven years before he was able to unite his country and set up his headquarters in Jerusalem (2 Samuel 5:4–5).

The 120 disciples waited in the upper room for several days between Jesus' ascension and the pouring out of His Spirit at Pentecost (Acts 1:1–14).

And this last example is a reminder of what He'd just recently said:

> Therefore keep watch, because you do not know on what day your Lord will come. But understand this: If the owner of the house had known at what time of night the thief was coming, he would have kept watch and would not have let his house be broken into. So you also must be ready, because the Son of Man will come at an hour when you do not expect him.
>
> Matthew 24:42–44

Today, *all* followers of Jesus are "waiting on the Lord" regarding His return. We are told to "be ready" so that, like Bilbo, we are in a position to reap the benefits when God fulfills His promise.

Continuing Themes

Once again, chapter 11 is among the shorter sections in *The Hobbit* and does not contain a lot of action or new information. However, several events do reinforce many of the primary themes and ideas we've been exploring.

I'll briefly highlight those events in the remaining pages of this chapter.

BILBO AS DIVINE AGENT

Recall that, early on, we saw Gandalf serve as an Agent of Providence in three distinct ways. As an Agent of Divine Initiation, the wizard set in motion several chains of events that would impact not just Thorin and Company but all of Middle-earth. As an Agent of Divine Wrath, Gandalf destroyed the forces of evil whenever he came into contact with them. And as an Agent of Divine Rescue, he repeatedly saved Bilbo and the dwarves from danger.

As the story progressed, Bilbo began to function within those roles, starting with the clash against the goblins in the Misty Mountains. When Gandalf left them on the borders of Mirkwood, Bilbo took his place as leader within the group *and* replaced Gandalf as an Agent of Providence.

In chapter 11, Tolkien lets us know in slightly subtle terms that Bilbo has indeed appropriated Gandalf's role within the story. When the dwarves are unable to open the mysterious back door, they begin to complain and suggest to each other that Bilbo walk through the front gate wearing his magic ring.

When Bilbo hears them, he notes that he's the one who has to get the dwarves out of their difficulties ever since Gandalf left.

But now his actions (in chapter 11 and beyond) will confirm his new position. As an Agent of Divine Initiation, he finds the path leading to the hidden door; he is also the only one to comprehend the runes on Thorin's map, and his quick thinking allows the dwarves to open the door once the keyhole is revealed. As an Agent of Divine Wrath, Bilbo will voluntarily walk down the tunnel to confront Smaug, and the thrush will carry his inside information to Bard, ultimately leading to Smaug's demise. And as an Agent of Divine Rescue, the hobbit will move the dwarves inside the tunnel before Smaug's sneak attack on the mountainside, again saving their lives.

The Last Temptation of Bilbo

At the start of this book, I recommended paying attention to moments when Bilbo pines for his old home (and old life) in the Shire. These are indicators that the hobbit is still working through the motives and cravings of his "old self." They're also signs that he is in danger of losing the focus and attention needed to succeed on his quest.

The most precarious of these occurrences now takes place as Bilbo sits on the grassy space between the locked door and the walls around—what he and the dwarves refer to as the "doorstep."

With his back against a rock, Bilbo knows the black wall of shadow he sees in the distance is Mirkwood. Beyond that, he can see the blue blur of the Misty Mountains—far, far away. He cannot see beyond that, but he knows that's where he would find the Shire if he decided to leave and go home.

For days, Bilbo sits with his back against that rock and broods about the Shire, about going home. This is the last time he toys with such temptation before the climax of his story—but make no mistake, he is tempted.

Fortunately for everyone, he resists long enough for Providence to step in and provide him with another opportunity to take action and save the day.

DIVINE ASSISTANCE

Just a quick review: We know from *The Silmarillion* and other works that Middle-earth was created by a divine being called Ilúvatar. We also know that Ilúvatar rarely takes direct action in the world, preferring to work through Divine Agents in order to make known his will and to see it carried out.

Most of his agents came from the ranks of the Valar and Maiar: the immortal, angel-like beings he sent into the world at its beginning. These were responsible for creating many of the geological structures within the world and were the primary teachers for the elves—the firstborn in Middle-earth.

In Bilbo's day, however, they have largely separated themselves from Middle-earth and dwell in Valinor, across the sea. For this reason, the Istari were sent into Middle-earth in order to help stewards and shape the events there. The Istari are all Maiar, lower angels; again, Gandalf is one of them.

There have been times throughout Middle-earth's history when mortal beings have been conscripted into service as Divine Agents. Tuor, father of Eärendil, is a good example. So is Bilbo Baggins. Initially chosen by Gandalf, throughout his adventure we've seen Bilbo develop into a true hero—a Divine Agent initiating events, bringing wrath upon evil, and rescuing those in need.

Now and again Bilbo has received divine assistance, including his dramatic rescue by the eagles and even his finding of the One Ring. However, nothing has been overt; nothing could be confirmed as supernatural.

Until chapter 11.

As Bilbo sits on the doorstep, looking west toward his home and enduring his darkest moment of temptation, he begins to feel like he's waiting for something. Then, hearing a sharp sound behind him, he turns to see a thrush knocking snails against the rock wall. Instantly he remembers the rune-letters from Thorin's map—"stand by the grey stone when the thrush knocks"[6]—and understands. Summoning the dwarves, they all watch as a last red burst of sunlight pushes through a gap in the clouds and lands upon the door, revealing a keyhole. Thorin is able to use the key that came with his map, and the door opens.

This is a supernatural occurrence by any standard. The overall event spans hundreds of years, from the making of the map to Bilbo's flash of realization on the doorstep. It incorporates specific times, weather patterns, lunar cycles, a bird, some snails, even the hobbit's inner thoughts.

It's a miracle, in other words. And it comes when Bilbo and the dwarves were at their lowest point, mired in frustration, uncertainty, and doubt.

12

Bilbo's Two Battles

With the hidden door unlocked, Bilbo and his friends are officially on the brink. All that's left to do is deal with Smaug, gather up the treasure, and find some way for Bilbo to carry it home. (All three tasks are easier said than done, as we'll soon see.)

But before we explore Bilbo's first encounter with the dragon, this seems a good time to step back and fully fathom just how far the hobbit has come.

Way back in chapter 1, Bilbo Baggins was confronted by individuals and ideas that seemed outrageous—not to mention dangerous.

Consider:

- He met Gandalf for the first time.
- He not only met Thorin and Company for the first time but had them barge into his house and bully him around for several hours.

- When Bilbo saw a fire outside his window that reminded him of a dragon, he became so frightened he attempted to hide behind his own beer barrels and hope the dwarves all went away.
- When Gandalf mentioned the possibility of never returning from the proposed journey, Bilbo let out a shriek and collapsed into a heap of nonsensical gibberish.

That's not an auspicious beginning for a hero-to-be, but, as the saying goes, "It's not how you start that matters, but how you finish." As we examine Bilbo Baggins here and now, we can say he is in the process of finishing well. Consider:

- He has replaced Gandalf as Agent of Divine Initiation, Wrath, and Rescue.
- He has replaced Thorin as leader within the company. He has even learned how to deal with Thorin's excessive style, such as when the would-be king starts to pontificate in front of the unlocked door.
- Whereas he once ran and hid at the *thought* of a dragon, he now is preparing to walk into Smaug's lair alone to scout out the situation. (He will, twice, in a span of less than twenty-four hours.)
- Instead of collapsing in fear at the prospect of death, repeatedly he has risked his life for the benefit of his friends. He's about to do so again by attempting detective work right under Smaug's nose.

Not bad! And yet—he has not finished. He still has two more battles to fight to fulfill his personal mission. Specifically, he will need to confront fear and pride in order to fully become the hero of his own story.

The Battle Against Fear

As he walks down the dwarf-carved tunnel, away from the sky and the stars, we can imagine Bilbo hoping against hope that he will find no dragon in the main chamber. We can also sense those hopes starting to fade when he sees a red glow at the end of the tunnel in front of him. We can envision those hopes dwindling further still as he feels the cold air become hot and vaporous. And we can feel those hopes evaporate altogether when he hears the vast gurgling clamor of a monstrous beast snoring in an unknown stage of sleep.

Accordingly, there are two things we know for certain as he freezes midstride and considers his situation: (1) Bilbo is sure Smaug is waiting for him at the end of the passageway, and (2) Bilbo is terrified to go on.

Yes, the hobbit is afraid. And because we've followed him throughout the entire journey, we cringe when we see it and feel it because we know he has struggled so much with fear in the past. What we need to remember, though, is that Bilbo's prior failures had not come about because he experienced the emotion of fear but because he had reacted poorly to it.

He was afraid when the three trolls captured him, for example, and his fear prevented him from taking appropriate actions (running away, or warning his friends of the danger). Yet he also experienced fear when confronted by the spider in Mirkwood, and, in that instance, the hobbit remained poised; despite his fear—rather than because he didn't feel it—he stepped up, moved forward, and destroyed a creature of evil.

This ability to do the right thing despite the presence of fear is the essence of courage. It's one of the areas in which Bilbo has experienced the most progress throughout his process of growth.

Back to the tunnel now, where Bilbo has a vital choice to make: Will he give in to fear and turn back, or he will press ahead and take his place among the heroes of Middle-earth? Tolkien makes it clear that Bilbo's internal struggle regarding this decision is *the* crucial moment in his battle against fear and its effects.

In the end, Bilbo chooses the path of heroism. He refuses to be controlled by his terror and instead embraces the right thing even though he is afraid—he wills, *determines*, to be courageous.

He chooses to go forward.

ᴛhe ᴮattle ᴀgainst ᴾride

Proverbs 16:18 is one of the best-known (and most often applied) verses in the Bible: "Pride goes before destruction, a haughty spirit before a fall."

That verse also lies at the core of Bilbo's second battle in chapter 12.

Having been victorious in his final confrontation with fear, Bilbo does indeed go down into the main chamber and witness Smaug's terrible majesty. More so, he witnesses the terrible beauty of the immense treasure, on top of which Smaug sleeps, piled around in massive heaps. Recalling why he was originally hired, Bilbo grabs a heavy golden cup and flees back up the tunnel.

As he makes his way back to the dwarves, we see that a seed of pride has already sprouted and is sending subtle tendrils toward his heart. He tells himself this will show the dwarves and that they will never again be able to label him a grocer instead of a burglar.

A Sinister Twist

Of course it's natural for Bilbo to be proud of his efforts, particularly of victory in the struggle against fear.

But already there is a sliver of something sinister in the hobbit's pride—something spiteful. His first thought after a successful mission is that it will make the dwarves sorry for what was said several months earlier.

This is the kind of pride the Bible warns about in several places:

> The Lord detests all the proud of heart.
> Be sure of this: They will not go unpunished.
>
> Proverbs 16:5

> To the arrogant I say, "Boast no more,"
> and to the wicked, "Do not lift up your horns.
> Do not lift your horns against heaven;
> do not speak so defiantly."
>
> Psalm 75:4–5

> Do nothing out of selfish ambition or vain conceit. Rather, in humility value others above yourselves, not looking to your own interests but each of you to the interests of the others.
>
> Philippians 2:3–4

> Live in harmony with one another. Do not be proud, but be willing to associate with people of low position. Do not be conceited.
>
> Romans 12:16

And this pride of Bilbo's does go before destruction. When Smaug sees the cup is missing, he bursts out of the front gate in wrath to scorch the mountain's western slope (and singeing the whole group.) The dwarves haul up Bofur and Bombur (and some supplies) by ropes, but the dragon chases down their ponies, leaving the entire company stranded on the mountainside.

Thorin and the others take stock of their situation the following morning, and quickly realize they have very few options to consider. They can't run away; any prospect of a frontal assault on Smaug seems more than foolish.

In the end, Bilbo volunteers for another trip down the tunnel to see if anything can be gained by another examination of the dragon.

THE SECOND BATTLE

Confrontation number two with Smaug is the frame for a second internal struggle in chapter 12—this time a battle against pride rather than fear.

We catch a few more "pride glimpses" before Bilbo even starts down the tunnel. His attitude toward the dwarves has become condescending. His manner of speaking with them has become truculent and rude. He goes so far as to wish he was back at home and had never joined the adventure.

Even his willingness to go down and re-inspect Smaug has become twisted. He makes the offer casually, almost flippantly. Listening to him, we begin to suspect he's become rather arrogant.

Those suspicions are quickly confirmed as Bilbo makes his way down. He feels proud at how silently he's walking. He sees only a dim glow from the inner chamber, and he convinces himself everything's okay—that Smaug is asleep and won't notice when the hobbit enters his chambers. He says, "Cheer up Bilbo!"[1]

When Bilbo last made this trek, he was so terrified he had to force himself to go on—and rightfully so. His life was in jeopardy. This time, the pendulum has swung in the opposite direction. Having gained some control over his fear, Bilbo overbalances and charges ahead with far too much self-confidence.

The absurdity of the situation would be comical if Bilbo

weren't risking his life (and the lives of his friends) in such a foolhardy manner. He believes he's safe because the dragon can't see him, but he doesn't realize—and doesn't take time to consider—that dragons have a keen sense of smell. Smaug can feel a change in the chamber's air when Bilbo peeps in from the tunnel's base.

In short, Smaug is aware the instant the intruder breaches his lair, and all that saves the hobbit from instant incineration is his magic ring.

After Smaug initiates a conversation, we learn something surprising: Bilbo knows how to speak with a dragon. Perhaps he learned this skill in conversation with the dwarves, or perhaps it's one of those extra qualities (along with telling riddles and throwing rocks at spiders) that Gandalf was aware of when he first recruited the hobbit.

In any case, Bilbo holds his own with Smaug—at first. He flatters the dragon and uses riddling talk to keep it guessing, which keeps him alive. Eventually, however, those seeds of pride cause the hobbit to overbalance once again; he is tricked by the dragon into revealing valuable information.

For example, Smaug confirms that Bilbo is part of a company of fourteen and that several of them are dwarves. He also confirms that they received help from the Lakemen in Esgaroth—a connection that spurs him to attack the city and ultimately destroy it. (Truly, pride does go before destruction.)

The hobbit obtains useful intelligence of his own when he spots a bald patch in the hollow of Smaug's left breast. And now, at this point, he wisely decides to leave. He has what he was looking for; he wants to return to the dwarves and see whether it can be put to use.

In his haughtiness, though, he's unable to forgo a verbal jab at the dragon, telling him that not only do ponies take some catching, but burglars do too. This inexcusable outburst of pride leaves him literally and figuratively burned.

EVALUATIONS

So how should we grade Mr. Baggins after these two major chapter 12 battles? From my perspective, most of his actions earn passing marks.

Bilbo overcame lifelong subservience to fear and demonstrated true bravery in the face of the unknown. He showed courage in his willingness to face Smaug again, and he successfully procured information that will lead to the dragon's eventual destruction.

At the same time, his brief dalliance with impudence and conceit nearly cost him far more than burnt skin and hurt feelings.

The silver lining from Bilbo's struggle with pride is that he recognized his mistakes—and learned from them. After barely escaping the flames of the dragon's wrath, Bilbo called himself a fool and notes sagely that one should never laugh at live dragons. He also got his head on straight about the company's overall status, reminding himself that he isn't nearly through this adventure yet.

The upshot is that Bilbo's humility is restored, and the valuable lessons he learns about the dangers of overconfidence will come in handy in the days that follow—especially in his decisions before the Battle of Five Armies.

Character Profile: Smaug

Smaug the dragon is one of the more enigmatic inhabitants of Tolkien's mythology. The specter of his power and past deeds dominates the beginning of *The Hobbit*, and it seems impossible that, whether with or without Bilbo, the dwarves will be able to dislodge the guardian of their treasure.

As the quest unfolds, the company encounters a host of other creatures and repeatedly are victorious, which gives us confidence in their abilities (and especially in Bilbo's).

Even so, behind it all, the monstrous dragon still looms. Each time they push through another obstacle or transcend a challenge, we can't help but think, *Yes, but how are they going to get past Smaug?* We fear him long before we ever see the Lonely Mountain.

THE HISTORY OF THE DRAGONS

Dragons play a small yet significant role in Tolkien's mythological history.

During his reign in Middle-earth, Melkor made Glaurung the father of dragons. It's not clear whether he created the first dragon on his own or if he corrupted an existing creature. Either way, Glaurung was a major force for evil's forces during Melkor's wars with the elves.

There are several similarities between Glaurung and Smaug, his descendent. Both dragons were fierce fighters. Glaurung was unleashed for the first time during the Dagor Bragollach or "Battle of Sudden Flame"—the fourth battle between Melkor and the elves. He was so powerful, and so unexpected in that conflict, that he almost singlehandedly broke the elves' siege around Angband.

Both Glaurung and Smaug also possessed a great deal of cunning, which they used to inflict harm on people whenever they could. *The Silmarillion* tells the story of Túrin Turumbar, a man whose life bore reflections of Oedipus. Túrin was a warrior who'd been separated from his family at an early age. Through the direct influence and intervention of Glaurung, Túrin ended up marrying his sister and inadvertently betraying those he cared most about. (He avenged himself in the end, however, by slaying the dragon with his sword.)

Finally, Glaurung was the first dragon to claim a horde of treasure and guard it jealously. He succeeded in this by destroying Nargothrond, an elvish stronghold in the caves, and gathering all its plunder for his bed. Smaug followed suit thousands of years later under the Lonely Mountain.

When the armies of the Valar came across the sea to finally break Melkor's strength and return him to Valinor for judgment, most of his forces were destroyed—including the dragons. Only a scattered few were left to trouble isolated pockets of the world.

By the time thirteen dwarves and a wizard visited Bilbo Baggins's house in the Shire, Smaug was the last great dragon still living.

A Literary History

Glaurung was not Smaug's only notable ancestor, however.

I've mentioned that J. R. R. Tolkien was an ardent fan of Norse mythology and of old stories from the northern regions. One piece of literature that held a particularly dear place in his heart was *Beowulf*—an ancient Old English poem that follows the adventures of the hero and his battles against three monsters.

When a terrible creature called Grendel begins attacking the mead hall of Hrothgar, King of the Danes, Beowulf arrives to help and succeeds in slaying the monster with his bare hands. Grendel's mother, enraged by her son's death, then attacks and also is killed by Beowulf, who follows her into an underwater lair.

Decades later, Beowulf has become king of his own people, the Geats. When yet another terrible dragon comes to scour the countryside, Beowulf slays it but is mortally wounded himself. The poem ends with an account of his funeral by the sea.

In an essay called "Beowulf: The Monsters and the Critics," Tolkien wrote the following about dragons as archetypes of literature:

> A dragon is no idle fancy. Whatever may be his origins, in fact or invention, the dragon in legend is a potent creation of men's imagination, richer in significance than his barrow is in gold. Even today (despite the critics) you may find men not ignorant of tragic legend and history, who have heard of heroes and indeed seen them, who yet have been caught by the fascination of the worm.[2]

Apparently he became such a man, for there's little doubt his depiction of the dragon Smaug is a literary tip of the cap to *Beowulf*'s unnamed worm.

Consider the similarities: *Beowulf*'s dragon was a winged, fire-breathing terror that lived in an abandoned stronghold and brooded over a hoard of treasure. In the story, someone sneaks into its lair and steals a gold cup. After the theft, the dragon bursts upon the countryside in a rage of flame and destruction. Beowulf is killed in the process of slaying it. (That's one reason Tolkien wrote about Bard's presumed death after Smaug was destroyed.)

All of these storylines have a reflection in Smaug. But as we'll see below, Smaug had other parts to play in *The Hobbit*.

SMAUG'S ROLE IN THIS SEGMENT OF THE STORY

Like all good villains, Smaug is (in literary terms) a dynamic character. He is a well-rounded creature of evil. This makes a contrast with the other evil beings in *The Hobbit*.

The trolls are violent and destructive, for example, but they don't possess many other qualities that make them more of a threat—say, cleverness or guile. On the other side, the goblins are known to be extremely crafty but don't pose much of a threat individually. They must come against opponents *en masse* before they are really dangerous.

Smaug himself is the total package—extremely destructive and endlessly cunning. As such, he reflects the Bible's two primary descriptions of evil.

First, consider Genesis 3:1–5:

> The serpent was more crafty than any of the wild animals the Lord God had made. He said to the woman, "Did God really say, 'You must not eat from any tree in the garden'?"
>
> The woman said to the serpent, "We may eat fruit from the trees in the garden, but God did say, 'You must not eat fruit from the tree that is in the middle of the garden, and you must not touch it, or you will die.'"
>
> "You will not certainly die," the serpent said to the woman. "For God knows that when you eat from it your eyes will be opened, and you will be like God, knowing good and evil."

The tempting serpent, crafty and beguiling, uses clever words and half-truths to weave a web of deceit around Eve and lure her in for destruction. Smaug's wiliness temporarily causes Bilbo to think the dwarves have been lying to him all along about his share of the treasure.

Second, take another look at 1 Peter 5:8:

> Be alert and of sober mind. Your enemy the devil prowls around like a roaring lion looking for someone to devour.

Evil is also destructive and is described by the apostle in connection with the most-feared beast of his time. Smaug reflects such destruction and personifies the concept of "looking for someone to devour."

All of that to say, Smaug's primary role in *The Hobbit* is to serve as a credible, convincing manifestation of evil and to highlight the horrible consequences such malevolence has upon the world.

13

The Seeds of Greed

Many things in this world can be measured without much difficulty—if you have the right instrument for the measuring.

Small distances can be calculated with a tape measure. Large distances can be measured with lasers and reflective lenses. If you want to find out how fast someone is driving, use a radar gun. If you want to determine how heavy something is, take your pick from any number of specialized scales designed for everything from a single bacteria to an elephant.

Other elements and aspects are not so easily quantified. For instance, one of the driving, behind-the-scenes questions in *The Hobbit* is how to measure a person's—or a hobbit's—moral character.

We readers can see that Bilbo Baggins has seen moral growth throughout his journey, but perhaps we look for a way to determine just how much he's been changed. Has he matured a little since the sudden party in Bag End? Has he been moderately reshaped? Is he a totally new creature?

Thus far Tolkien has used fear—or, more precisely, he has used Bilbo's *reactions* to fear—as a plumb rod to gauge the hobbit's development. When we set Bilbo against that rod during his contacts with Smaug, we can definitively say that he has been profoundly changed. In fact, we can say he has conquered his tendency to be controlled by fear and has become a truly heroic figure.

And so Tolkien's instrument for measuring moral character now changes, starting in chapter 13. From this point he will use money, of all things, as a way to establish the moral fiber of different characters—including Bilbo.

Smaug's huge hoard of plunder becomes a shining scale that pegs one as greedy or generous, as foolish or wise, as morally deficient or morally strong.

Three Assessments

In later chapters, Tolkien will use Smaug's vast trove to evaluate the quality of other, more minor characters such as Bard the Bowman, the Master of Lake-town, Thranduil (king of the wood elves in Mirkwood), and more.

To start things off, though, he utilizes chapters 12 and 13 to reveal the mettle and motives of Smaug, the dwarves, and Bilbo.

Assessing Smaug

Not surprisingly, Smaug the dragon scores a zero on his character assessment. He is the personification of malice, cruelty, cunning, and greed.

The irony is that Smaug has absolutely no use for money. He purchases nothing; he needs no kind of savings or means of investment. For all intents and purposes, the dragon is a beast that lives off the land.

Similarly, there's no evidence within the story that Smaug is fond of the treasure over which he has so long presided. There are no mentions of appreciating a particular jewel's beauty or even feeling happy about the quantity of riches in which he's immersed—only that he broods over every detail of his plunder and has complete, ongoing awareness of its inventory.

What Smaug does radiate is a burning desire to possess. In his extreme greed he ravaged the kingdom under the mountain and the town of Dale, then piled the wealth of others in titanic heaps for an elaborate bed within his lair. His pleasure stems only in knowing that he possesses it while others do not.

These traits result in one of the few moments throughout Tolkien's entire legendarium where he risks breaking the story's spell to make a moral point.

When Smaug discovers the golden cup is missing, he bursts through the gate in wrath. The dragon's state is described as the kind of rage only seen when rich people who have more than they can enjoy suddenly lose something they've long possessed but seldom used. For Tolkien, such a tone is almost preachy, and it shows how strongly he felt about the matter.

Once again he reflects the sentiments of several biblical authors, including James:

> Now listen, you rich people, weep and wail because of the misery that is coming on you. Your wealth has rotted, and moths have eaten your clothes. Your gold and silver are corroded. Their corrosion will testify against you and

eat your flesh like fire. You have hoarded wealth in the last days. Look! The wages you failed to pay the workers who mowed your fields are crying out against you. The cries of the harvesters have reached the ears of the Lord Almighty. You have lived on earth in luxury and self-indulgence. You have fattened yourselves in the day of slaughter. You have condemned and murdered the innocent one, who was not opposing you.

James 5:1–6

The hoarding of wealth, abominable at any time, is especially so in the presence of others in need. Unfortunately, some of the characters we have appreciated thus far are about to display Smaug-like attitudes and actions.

Assessing the Dwarves

If Thorin and the dwarves had a "life verse," I'm afraid it would be this:

Those who want to get rich fall into temptation and a trap and into many foolish and harmful desires that plunge people into ruin and destruction. For the love of money is a root of all kinds of evil. Some people, eager for money, have wandered from the faith and pierced themselves with many griefs.

1 Timothy 6:9–10

Yes, the dwarves have been "decent enough fellows" during their adventures from Bag End to the Lonely Mountain. They've exuded stiffness and grumpiness at times, sure, along with a bit of haughtiness on Thorin's part. But Bilbo has called them his friends, and we readers feel the same way.

Yet from the moment they encounter Smaug's treasure, things change. To start, the word *foolish* becomes appropriate to describe their actions.

When they can stand the darkness and heat of the tunnel no longer, Thorin and Company make a desperate escape attempt, passing down into Smaug's lair. Amazingly, they find no waiting dragon. But instead of blessing Providence for their luck and hastily retreating, they fall into temptation and a trap when they see the treasure. Utterly mesmerized, they linger a long while in the most dangerous place imaginable.

Some of the dwarves begin stuffing their pockets with gold and jewels. Others wander around the tremendous lode, reminiscing about artifacts they remember from times long ago. Fili and Kili grab harps and strike up a tune!

Bilbo finally puts an end to the madness by reminding them that they don't know where Smaug is, and he could return at any moment. Only then do the dwarves gradually, grudgingly leave the treasure to save their own lives.

Yet the damage has been done. In the days ahead, the planted seeds of greed will reap terrible consequences—including "ruin and destruction." Some dwarves will even find themselves literally "pierced" with griefs.

Assessing Bilbo

If you've paid attention, you probably noticed a pattern developing with the "three assessments" in this section. Smaug is at one end of the spectrum as the personification of greed; the dwarves are toward the middle as decent beings corrupted by the love of money; so Bilbo must be at the other end of the spectrum, generous and devoid of avarice—right?

While that's the eventual reality, things don't look promising at the start.

In chapter 12, Bilbo caught the first glimpse of Smaug's treasure after descending the tunnel and winning the victory over his fear. He was blown away. In fact, there were "no words left to express his staggerment."[1]

This is understandable, given the hoard's immensity. But what happens inside Bilbo's mind and heart when he sees it is disconcerting to say the least. He ruminates on the "lust" and "glory" of such treasure, and his heart is "filled and pierced" with the "desire of dwarves."[2] This is all bad news, of course, and the word *pierced* should catch our attention given what we read from 1 Timothy 6.

But just as disturbing is the way Bilbo stands motionless as he gazes at the treasure, almost forgetting the terrible dragon just a few feet in front of him! Indeed, Bilbo's fear of Smaug decreasing because of his desire for the treasure is a foreshadowing of the dwarves' foolishness in chapter 13.

Two things are clear in this encounter. First, Bilbo is experiencing a legitimate temptation. Having just conquered his fear, the hobbit is beset by a new peril—a new chance to make the right choice and grow stronger or make the wrong choice and fail both himself and his friends.

Second, Tolkien is setting up a comparison between Bilbo and his companions. The hobbit and the dwarves have the same initial reaction to the treasure—amazement, desire, and a thoughtless lack of awareness. Over time, however, Bilbo and the dwarves will take entirely different views (and actions) when it comes to the pull of wealth.

In fact, Bilbo begins to separate from the dwarves as soon as chapter 13, when the company escapes through the vacant lair. While the dwarves are just getting warmed up with grabbing for jewels and reminiscing about long-forgotten riches, the hobbit's desire for amassing spoils quickly fades.

Remember: He pulls the dwarves out of their folly by reminding them that Smaug could return at any moment. And instead of gathering gold to carry, he muses that he would give up a whole stack of precious goblets if he could get a drink of something cheerful from one of Beorn's wooden bowls.

These examples show that Bilbo is reestablishing a proper priority when it comes to riches, and this will serve him well in the days to come.

THE ARKENSTONE

Bilbo *does* stuff one jewel into his pocket in chapter 13: the Arkenstone.

Described by Thorin as the "heart of the mountain" and one of the most striking gems ever discovered, Bilbo comes across it while exploring the main hall seeking any signs of Smaug's whereabouts. He finds no dragon, of course, but is instead drawn forward by a strange, dim light.

After discovering the Arkenstone, Bilbo's arm suddenly shoots out as if drawn by some enchantment of the jewel. He even closes his eyes while he pockets the stone—as if he doesn't want to see what his hand is doing.

At this point, there's no doubt the hobbit intends to keep the Arkenstone for himself. He reasons that Thorin said he could choose from the treasure for his one-fourteenth share, and he wants the Arkenstone more than all else combined.

The problem is that Bilbo knows Thorin feels the same way. And he even thinks to himself that trouble will come of his actions when eventually he tells the dwarves what he did.

The entire episode is puzzling. The frequent mention of Bilbo being "drawn" to the stone and experiencing its "enchantment" makes it seem like outside forces are at work—we get the impression that his taking of the jewel is a key moment but can't yet say whether the results will be for good or evil.

We are left with questions: Does Bilbo's taking of the Arkenstone mean that the "seeds of greed" are growing in his heart as well as in the dwarves'? Do the outside forces working upon Bilbo represent Providence or something more sinister? Is Bilbo right that there will be consequences for his actions?

All these queries and more will be addressed in the chapters to come.

The Twisting of the Dwarves

Before turning to Smaug's fate, I want to make one thing clear on the dwarves' predilection toward greed and love of money. Namely, that their penchant is not a natural condition; it's not who the dwarves were created to be.

I understand that it's easy to assume otherwise. The dwarves are connected with money and covetousness so often throughout Tolkien's mythology that we can begin to feel like they have no choice in the matter. Even when dwarves commit despicable acts in the name of greed, there is a part of us that may think, *That's just what dwarves do. They can't help it.*

Thoughts like these are incorrect, however, because they are inconsistent with the earliest history of the dwarves as a race within Middle-earth.

As I mentioned in chapter 10, the dwarves were originally created by Aulë, a member of the Valar. This angel-like being had a love of mining and smithwork, and he created the dwarves because he wanted to share his knowledge with others who could emulate and refine his craft.

However, in *The Silmarillion*, Tolkien emphasizes that Aulë's moral character takes delight in making rather than hoarding things.[3]

He was more likely to be generous with treasure than to keep it for himself. Therefore, he did not impart any measure of greed or covetousness into the earliest dwarves. Nor did those dwarves learn such qualities from his example or teaching.

Rather, the faults demonstrated by later generations—including that of Thorin and Company—are the result of a gradual corruption arising from the love of money. Like all demonstrations of evil in Middle-earth, their greed was caused by the twisting of something originally created to be good.

This twisting will play prominently in the final events of *The Hobbit*, and will include major consequences for those who choose to wallow in their corruption rather than resisting evil and striving to once again become who they were created to be.

14

Whispers and Flame

If any doubt J. R. R. Tolkien's mettle as a literary crafts-man, they need only look to his handling of Smaug's destruction in order to correct their mistake.

In chapter 12, the dragon tricked Bilbo into revealing that he and the dwarves were assisted by the men of Esgaroth (Lake-town). Smashing the hidden door with a huge blow from his tail (trapping Bilbo and the dwarves inside), Smaug set his sights on the Running River and sped south to remind the men of the Lake who is the true King under the Mountain.

The image we're left with at chapter's end is terrifying: the dragon hurtling in rage toward Esgaroth with death and destruction in his wake.

Diving into chapter 13, however, we don't find out right away what happened during the ensuing confrontation.

The chapter's middle doesn't tell us either—nor does its end. We're given a look at Bilbo and the dwarves as they explore his lair, but we see or hear nothing from Smaug himself.

Tolkien, by making us wait an entire chapter before returning to the scene, effectively ratchets up the tension. He puts us on pins and needles.

This sensation is enhanced by the uncertainty of Bilbo and the dwarves: within Smaug's lair, at the gate, and then outside the Lonely Mountain. The more they ponder where the dragon has gone and when (if at all) he'll be coming back, the more we ponder with them.

Thankfully, we do get answers in chapter 14—and are not disappointed. The clash in Esgaroth is as action-packed as we could have imagined. And yet, surprisingly, the crucial moment involves more subtlety than strength.

An Apt Allusion

Another highly appreciable element about Tolkien is his ability to incorporate biblical and historical allusions without being obvious or heavy-handed. The final confrontation between Smaug and Bard is an excellent example.

Specifically, Bard's interaction with the old thrush is a powerfully suggestive allusion to Elijah's encounter with God in 1 Kings 19:

> The Lord said, "Go out and stand on the mountain in the presence of the Lord, for the Lord is about to pass by."
> Then a great and powerful wind tore the mountains apart and shattered the rocks before the Lord, but the Lord was not in the wind. After the wind there was an earthquake, but the Lord was not in the earthquake. After the earthquake came a fire, but the Lord was not in the

fire. And after the fire came a gentle whisper. When Elijah heard it, he pulled his cloak over his face and went out and stood at the mouth of the cave.

vv. 11–13

Elijah was a noted prophet to the people of Israel between 900 and 850 BC. His ministry regularly brought him into conflict with King Ahab and Queen Jezebel because of their preference for Baal worship.

Elijah is most famous for his confrontation with the prophets of Baal on Mount Carmel, where he used fire called down from heaven to show that Yahweh is the only and true God. What he experienced in this cave also is memorable, for on this rarest of occasions a human was permitted to stand in the presence of God and live.

In order to have such an unparalleled experience, Elijah needed to discern God's voice in the midst of chaos—and that is why Tolkien created a link between Elijah and Bard the Bowman.

The language describing Smaug's attack hints at such a connection:

- *"The Lord was not in the wind."* We hear the roar of the dragon's approach, with emphasis on the terrible beating of its wings.
- *"The Lord was not in the earthquake."* Smaug smashes several buildings with his tail; the entire town is leveled by his death throes.
- *"The Lord was not in the fire."* Smaug liberally uses fire, his primary weapon, while assaulting the town.

But it's through the old thrush that Tolkien solidifies the link between Bard and Elijah. Amid chaos and destruction, the bird alights on Bard's shoulder and speaks vital information into his ear. The thrush is an echo of that "gentle whisper" Elijah heard after the wind and earthquake and fire.

More, the thrush is an Agent of Providence. It serves as Agent of Divine Initiation when it tells Bard about Smaug's weak spot and advises him where and when to shoot his final arrow. It serves as Agent of Divine Wrath in that its advice directly results in the destruction of the most powerful evil creature in the story. And it serves as Agent of Divine Rescue in that its actions save the majority of the townspeople in Esgaroth from certain death.

To summarize, Tolkien used one of the most important moments in *The Hobbit* to point toward one of the most important moments in the Old Testament. Surrounded by wind and fire and shaking ground, Bard the Bowman heeded the still, small voice of Providence—and saved the day.

Weakness and Strength

These verses bear repeating when we look at the events of chapter 14:

> God chose the foolish things of the world to shame the wise; God chose the weak things of the world to shame the strong. God chose the lowly things of this world and the despised things—and the things that are not—to nullify the things that are, so that no one may boast before him.

> 1 Corinthians 1:27–29

Smaug the dragon is unquestionably the strongest creature to appear in *The Hobbit*. And even if his wisdom is tainted by deception, he nevertheless is wise. It's this combination of intelligence and might that makes him so formidable as a servant of evil.

Yet despite his physical clout and intellectual acuity, he was destroyed in the end by the motley crew of a hobbit, a bird, and a man with an arrow.

Working alone, none could have put a dent in Smaug's defenses. And even working together they would seem an insufficient force to confront a creature that had wiped out entire cities. But in the Creator's service, these three woven-together strands of good produce something truly formidable.

I want to highlight one more example from this theme before addressing the concept of leadership in Middle-earth.

Given what we know about Bard and his role in slaying Smaug, the way he is presented at the beginning of this chapter is curious. For several pages he is referenced only as the man with the "grim voice" or the "grim-voiced man."[1] More, he is mocked by his fellow townspeople like a kind of grumpy outcast.

Why? Especially given what we learn later about Bard's lineage—he descends from Girion, King of Dale—why is our first impression so negative?

The answer points back again to a just-mentioned principle: the foolish will shame the wise; the weak will shame the strong. Tolkien intentionally paints Bard as a have-not within Esgaroth—especially when compared to someone like Lake-town's Master—in order that his heroism and leadership will point back to Providence as their source.

Leadership Lessons From Middle-Earth

Tolkien uses *The Hobbit*'s final chapters to keynote certain spiritual and moral themes. One, again, is the temptation of wealth. Another is leadership.

Several characters are given a chance to step into the breach as leaders during the story's final adventures. Some account themselves honorably; others expose their flaws and corruptions. Either way, Tolkien utilizes their decisions and actions to make statements about what it means to lead well, and why such leadership truly matters.

Looking specifically at chapter 14, the action revolves around three characters. One is Smaug, though as a solitary creature he doesn't demonstrate much leadership. The others are Bard and the Master of Esgaroth.

Tolkien has a lot to say about leadership through these two men. In fact, he often sets them side-by-side to directly compare the differences between their moral fiber and styles of leadership.

Let's see what he would have us learn through this pairing.

TRUE LEADERS DEMONSTRATE COURAGE

The virtue of courage represents the greatest disparity between Bard and the Master of Esgaroth. The former demonstrates courage in spades, while the latter wallows in buckets of cowardice.

Smaug's raid on the town effectively shines a spotlight on this difference.

Shortly after the dragon's arrival, the Master hops aboard his "great gilded boat,"[2] hoping to abandon Laketown unnoticed during the commotion and confusion.

Just two paragraphs later comes the description of Bard's valorous acts. Surrounded by flames, he stands firm to the last arrow while leading a company of archers in defending the town. His efforts are rewarded when Smaug is vanquished.

Proverbs 28:1 offers an apt summary: "The wicked flee

though no one pursues, but the righteous are as bold as a lion."

And the Bible has a lot to say about courage. Many great men and women of faith are also noted for their heroism—people like Joshua, Gideon, Deborah, and Daniel. Certainly David's victory over Goliath comes to mind when we consider Bard's confrontation with the dragon.

But many of Scripture's most audacious moments have nothing to do with battle or bloodshed. Esther's decision to put her life in the hands of King Xerxes and plead for the fate of her people demonstrated extreme bravery. The Bible especially emphasizes those who courageously face their own sinfulness and repent—again, like David after his affair with Bathsheba.

True Leaders Are Selfless

After Esgaroth is destroyed, the people gather together on the shores of the Long Lake. They are homeless and weary and distraught. Unfortunately, they receive no comfort from their elected leader.

The Master likewise is homeless and weary and distraught. And those are the primary matters he seeks to rectify in the hours after the conflict.

While the people had no shelter during the night's bitter cold, the Master did. Most of the people went hungry; the Master called loudly for men to bring him fire and food. While the townspeople suffered, the Master thought only of himself.

The Master's acts and attitude represent a dreadful leadership void—as Tolkien intended. They also provide a useful foil for Bard's selfless exploits.

While the Master demanded assistance, Bard organized survivors along the lakefront. While the Master was procuring shelter against the cold of the night, Bard tended to the sick and wounded.

Bard even goes so far as to undertake these actions in the Master's name. He is noble to the point of avoiding recognition for his good leadership.

In all this he reflects these words of Jesus:

> You know that those who are regarded as rulers of the Gentiles lord it over them, and their high officials exercise authority over them. Not so with you. Instead, whoever wants to become great among you must be your servant, and whoever wants to be first must be slave of all. For even the Son of Man did not come to be served, but to serve, and to give his life as a ransom for many.
>
> Mark 10:42–45

The most selfless aspect of Bard's leadership was his willingness to put his life on the line in defense of Esgaroth. He was willing to die to save others—which again reflects the priorities of Christ:

> My command is this: Love each other as I have loved you. Greater love has no one than this: to lay down one's life for one's friends.
>
> John 15:12–13

True Leaders Accept Responsibility

These actions of the Master are somewhat lethargic, but he does expend bursts of energy in an effort to accomplish two goals. The first is his attempt to escape during Smaug's attack. The second is his attempt to defend his actions by deflecting blame.

The people of Lake-town are understandably upset about his desertion and understandably impressed by Bard's demonstrations of altruism and courage. Therefore, finding Bard alive after the battle, they cry out against the Master and shout for Bard to become their king.

Despite his impotence against the dragon, the Master rises in defense of his own position. He starts by recommending that Bard go back to Dale if he wants to rule something—but this only increases the people's ire.

So he switches tactics. Instead of taking responsibility for his actions and seeking forgiveness, he works to shift blame from himself and toward Thorin and Company. That serves only to confirm our view of him as a career politician concerned only with his elevated status.

In contrast, Bard sensibly checks the people's fury against the dwarves, noting that Thorin and his companions are probably dead already and that the people of the lake have much more pressing problems to solve.

The fact that they *are* alive does not diminish the wisdom in his words. And as we'll see, such wisdom is in short supply with the dwarves.

15

The King
Under the Mountain

Most people today have very little to do with kings and queens. With the exception of Great Britain and a few isolated monarchies, much of the world has been split into democracies and dictatorships. This is a relatively new phenomenon: For many prior thousands of years, groups of people both large and small were governed by successive generations of royal families.

That also is true of almost all the people recorded in the Bible, whether their rulers had the title of *King* or *Pharaoh* or *Caesar*. Therefore, maintaining an awareness of kingdoms and their leaders is necessary for a proper understanding of the Scriptures—as it is of Middle-earth.

Bloodlines

I want to say upfront that J. R. R. Tolkien was neither dismissive of nor antagonistic toward what we would think of as the "common man." Tolkien was a commoner himself, not being part of any royal family.

Nor did Tolkien believe ordinary people were incapable of leadership or of shaping the events of history. He believed quite the opposite, in fact, as is evident in Bilbo's accomplishments and in how Tolkien's stories regularly feature the weak shaming the strong (1 Corinthians 1:27–29).

However, it is clear from his books, including *The Hobbit*, that he did place a special emphasis on royalty. The members of his royal families possess an extra measure of dignity, esteem, and skill in a variety of abilities. Kings, queens, and their descendants are often more courageous in combat, more eloquent of speech, more filled with wisdom, and so on.

For instance, in *The Lord of the Rings*, Aragorn, lost heir of the kings of Númenor, is among the greatest warriors of his time and a gifted healer. He even has the strength of mind to strive with Sauron using the Palantír. Éowyn, daughter of Théoden, king of Rohan, is a fierce warrior. Boromir and Faramir, the sons of Denethor, Steward of Gondor, also are descendants of the Númenórian kings. The brothers are skilled fighters and eloquent speakers.

We should not be surprised by the inherent value Tolkien placed on men and women of noble birth. After all, he was a citizen of Great Britain, throughout his life a subject of monarchs. Further, he was a member of the British army during the reign of King George V.

Again, emphasis on royal lineage is also prevalent in Scripture. David and Solomon are the best-known examples, but frequently throughout the Old Testament,

God worked directly through the royal families of Israel and Judah.

And the New Testament makes it clear that the ancient bloodlines of God's people pointed to the world's true Sovereign:

> God, the blessed and only Ruler, the King of kings and Lord of lords, who alone is immortal and who lives in unapproachable light, whom no one has seen or can see. To him be honor and might forever. Amen.
>
> 1 Timothy 6:15–16

Bloodlines in The Hobbit

There are two reasons I want to highlight Tolkien's elevated estimation of kings, queens, and their progeny.

The first reason is that the adventures within *The Hobbit* reflect this perspective by emphasizing several characters with royal bloodlines.

Thorin is a descendant of Durin, one of the earliest fathers of the dwarves and the rightful King under the Mountain. The Lord of the Eagles plays a central role in rescuing the company from certain doom in the Misty Mountains and also saves the day by leading the eagles into the Battle of Five Armies. Thranduil, king of the wood elves, indirectly rescues the company from starvation in Mirkwood and shows great kindness to the people of Esgaroth after their town is destroyed by Smaug. As a descendant of Girion, Bard the dragon-slayer is rightful heir of the kingdom of Dale next to the Lonely Mountain. Even most of the action involving the goblins revolves around royalty (such as it is) with the Great Goblin and Bolg.

Again, by no means are these the only characters of note within *The Hobbit*. But it's clear that Tolkien wants

Middle-earth's upper-crust members present and active when major events are taking place.

The second (and more important) reason is to take a deeper look at the story's "primary royal": Thorin Oakenshield, King under the Mountain.

A Fallen Hero

When we first meet Thorin way back at the beginning, he is described as "an enormously important dwarf."[1] The other dwarves all submit to his leadership, and even Gandalf treats him with a notable measure of respect.

There are times where it really seems he has earned such treatment.

Sure, at certain moments Thorin behaves pompously, even haughtily. But other times the veil is peeled away and we glimpse something deeper and more powerful within the heart and spirit of the king—something noble.

Thorin's bravery against the trolls is a good example. After Bilbo's failure as a burglar (and as a hero), Thorin singlehandedly takes on three trolls in an effort to rescue his people. We also catch the foretaste of a quiet dignity during Thorin's interrogation by the king of the wood elves in Mirkwood. And when he reveals himself to the people of Lake-town during the Master's feast, he commands attention and obedience through sheer force of will—even while he's still dripping and bedraggled from his barrel-ride out of Mirkwood.

All of these factors and happenings help us see that Thorin Oakenshield has the potential to be a strong and wise king for his people.

Sadly, this potential is never realized. And in the end, all those hints of something noble in him only heighten the tragedy of his corruption and fall.

The seeds of that corruption were planted in chapter 13,

when the dwarves first beheld the awesome treasure. But they come to flower in chapter 15. More accurately, Thorin's greed comes into full bloom and causes him to make decisions that are both foolish and destructive.

Two Symptoms of Greed

Two symptoms best reveal Thorin's growing greed and corruption. The first is a continuation of the madness that overcame the dwarves in chapter 13.

Remember that when the dwarves first encountered the treasure, they were ignorant of Smaug's fate. They didn't know he had been killed, and they expected him to come swooping back under the mountain at any moment. Even so, their lust caused them to linger a long while in the main hall, stuffing their pockets and even singing songs in their mirth.

It took Bilbo's stern words to help Thorin come to his senses and order a retreat. But their thoughtlessness is repeated on a larger scale when the dwarves learn of Smaug's destruction—and of the armies currently on the march toward the Lonely Mountain.

Incredibly, Thorin decides to make a stand and fight. He doesn't seem to care that only a dozen dwarves (plus Mr. Baggins) are in the mountain with him. His plan is for a company of fourteen to withstand the might of two armies and to come out victorious.

His foolishness is intensified when Bard arrives and makes known his requests. He proposes that Thorin relinquish a twelfth-part of the treasure to cover what Smaug stole from Dale during his original attack on the mountain. Bard also asks—*not demands*—that the dwarves make a contribution to the people of Esgaroth who lost everything in the carnage of Smaug's last assault.

The proposal is more than fair; it would allow the dwarves to retain the vast majority of the treasure. More, it would allow them to retain their lives, which should have been tempting, besieged as they were on all sides.

Incredibly, Thorin refuses. In avaricious insanity he will risk his life—and those of his companions—to keep his fingers on every last jewel and coin.

Once again, Thorin and the dwarves serve as a vivid example of the many biblical warnings against the desire for wealth:

> Those who want to get rich fall into temptation and a trap and into many foolish and harmful desires that plunge people into ruin and destruction. For the love of money is a root of all kinds of evil. Some people, eager for money, have wandered from the faith and pierced themselves with many griefs.

1 Timothy 6:9–10

This attitude points to the second symptom of Thorin's greed. Namely, he and the other dwarves begin to resemble Smaug the dragon.

Think about it. For decades, Smaug brooded over the treasure in his lair under the Lonely Mountain. He was unable to spend it or use it in any way, but he hoarded it. He obsessed over every piece of gold and reacted in violent rage whenever anyone deigned to threaten what he claimed as his own.

Now think about Thorin. He and the dwarves are surrounded by two armies and so have no means of using the treasure. And yet they decide to stockpile it all for themselves. They spend their time admiring and cataloguing every facet of their wealth. And when Bard's messengers formally request a portion, Thorin reacts in furious rage, firing an arrow into an envoy's shield.

Far from resembling the noble king he was meant to be, Thorin takes on the traits of the very monster that long had tormented him and his people.

In this, he becomes the epitome of greed's corrupting power:

> When tempted, no one should say, "God is tempting me."
> God cannot be tempted by evil, nor does he tempt anyone;
> but each person is tempted when they are dragged away
> by their own evil desire and enticed. Then, after desire
> has conceived, it gives birth to sin; and sin, when it is
> full-grown, gives birth to death.
>
> James 1:13–15

The treasure was Thorin's temptation. He had pondered it for so long; he wanted it desperately. And his desire for wealth allows him to be dragged away from his life's purpose—to be his people's wise and noble leader. Greed leads Thorin to all kinds of sins that, in the end, will give birth to his death.

As the King Goes . . .

The regrettable reality of the situation is that Thorin's actions do not affect Thorin alone. Rather, as the King under the mountain becomes more and more degraded and despoiled, the same happens to his subjects.

After spurning Bard's herald by firing an arrow into his shield, he becomes so grim that the other dwarves dare not question him—he won't listen even to those who had risked their lives with him and for him on the long journey.

Even more surprising is that the other dwarves concur. Only Fili, Kili, and fat Bombur seem to understand that anything is wrong. The others have followed their king in his lust for the treasure, and thus they share in his corruption, stubbornness, violence, and uncertain future.

In this way, Tolkien crafted Thorin and his subjects so as to parallel the nations and kings of the Old Testament.

The great wisdom of Solomon, Israel's last great ruler, helped expand the kingdom's borders, wealth, and power to its pinnacle. Near the beginning of his reign, God gave him the following promises and warnings:

> If you walk before me faithfully with integrity of heart and uprightness, as David your father did, and do all I command and observe my decrees and laws, I will establish your royal throne over Israel forever, as I promised David your father when I said, "You shall never fail to have a successor on the throne of Israel."
>
> But if you or your descendants turn away from me and do not observe the commands and decrees I have given you and go off to serve other gods and worship them, then I will cut off Israel from the land I have given them and will reject this temple I have consecrated for my Name. Israel will then become a byword and an object of ridicule among all peoples.

1 Kings 9:4–7

Note how the actions of Solomon and his descendants connect to the entire nation. If he or his descendants drifted into sin and rebellion, then Israel would be cut off from the land and from God's favor—all God's people would experience negative consequences of the kings' transgressions.

Tragically, that's how things turned out, historically. After Solomon's death, the kingdom was split into two nations: Israel and Judah. And of the thirty-nine kings who ruled over them, only eight were righteous. The rest worshiped false gods—and led the Israelites into the same evil.

As a result, both were conquered—Israel by Assyria, Judah by Babylon—and most of the people in both nations were taken captive into foreign lands.

Thorin's guidance likewise results in high cost to himself and his people.

More Leadership Lessons From Middle-Earth

Thorin's actions in chapter 15 are a far cry from noble leadership, yet as with the Master of Esgaroth, we can glean valuable lessons from negative examples.

Specifically, we can explore two aspects of Tolkien's views on good leadership in light of Thorin's attitudes and actions.

True Leaders Take Wise Counsel

Proverbs 15:22 says, "Plans fail for lack of counsel, but with many advisers they succeed." This principle is played out again and again in the lives of the Old Testament kings.

One reason David was a great king was his willingness to surround considered advice from "outsiders," such as Nathan the prophet.

Thorin is not such a leader. When he hears of Smaug's ruin from Roäc—the leader of the great ravens who still live near the Lonely Mountain and can speak to other races—he (like the other dwarves) is overjoyed by the news.

But then Roäc tells him about the events that followed the dragon's death, including the march of the armies from Esgaroth and Mirkwood. Roäc concludes by offering three pieces of advice: He (1) reminds Thorin that thirteen is a small remnant of Durin's folk with which to wage a war; (2) encourages Thorin to trust Bard, who killed Smaug, rather than the Master of Lake-town; and (3) advises Thorin to take advantage of the chance to make peace among dwarves, men, and elves—even if it requires much gold.

This excellent advice is filled with commonsense guidance and inside information. However, Thorin refuses to listen, instead wanting messengers sent to nearby settlements of dwarves that might come to aid him in his war.

This entire conversation is juxtaposed with the earlier interaction between Bard and the thrush. Bard listened to wise counsel and changed his actions accordingly—thereby effecting Smaug's downfall.

TRUE LEADERS SHOW COMPASSION

King David himself is proof that no leader is perfect. *All* make mistakes. But the best ones acknowledge missteps and seek to rectify them. More, they understand that everyone errs, and so they learn to demonstrate compassion.

Because David was aware of his own faults, he was able to show mercy to those who wronged him—even, for instance, when his own son (Absalom) attempted to wrestle away his throne.

Also, most significantly, David had experienced compassion from God:

> The Lord is compassionate and gracious,
> slow to anger, abounding in love.
> He will not always accuse,
> nor will he harbor his anger forever;
> he does not treat us as our sins deserve
> or repay us according to our iniquities.
> For as high as the heavens are above the earth,
> so great is his love for those who fear him;
> as far as the east is from the west,
> so far has he removed our transgressions from us.
>
> Psalm 103:8–12

We've already highlighted how Bard demonstrated compassion on his people after the destruction of Esgaroth. Thranduil, king of the wood elves, shows even greater compassion by changing his course away from the Lonely Mountain and instead stopping to provide comfort and support to Lake-town.

Demonstrating true compassion, both leaders are blessed because of it.

Thorin, on the other hand, demonstrates no compassion whatsoever. He even mocks Bard for mentioning the people of the Lake being in dire need—the same people who cared for Bilbo and the dwarves after their harrowing journey out of Mirkwood. Thorin's coldness evokes Proverbs 11:24–26 when he goes so far as to say that he has no responsibility to help others just because the same monster that harmed him also happened to harm them:

> One person gives freely, yet gains even more;
> another withholds unduly, but comes to poverty.
> A generous person will prosper;
> whoever refreshes others will be refreshed.
> People curse the one who hoards grain,
> but they pray God's blessing on the one who is willing to sell.

Showing cruelty instead of compassion, Thorin reveals yet another flaw in his role as a leader—a flaw he and his people will pay for in days to come.

16

A Shrewd Hobbit

The four New Testament Gospels contain dozens of parables spoken by Jesus Christ. (A parable is a short story that teaches a practical or moral lesson.)

Many, such as the good Samaritan and the prodigal son, are famous for their ethical and spiritual impact throughout the world. Famous or not, most of these stories are easy to tell, easy to understand, and easy to apply.

There is one, however, that has baffled readers since it was first recorded. It's called the parable of the shrewd manager:

> There was a rich man whose manager was accused of wasting his possessions. So he called him in and asked him, "What is this I hear about you? Give an account of your management, because you cannot be manager any longer."

The manager said to himself, "What shall I do now? My master is taking away my job. I'm not strong enough to dig, and I'm ashamed to beg—I know what I'll do so that, when I lose my job here, people will welcome me into their houses."

So he called in each one of his master's debtors. He asked the first, "How much do you owe my master?"

"Nine hundred gallons of olive oil," he replied.

The manager told him, "Take your bill, sit down quickly, and make it four hundred and fifty."

Then he asked the second, "And how much do you owe?"

"A thousand bushels of wheat," he replied.

He told him, "Take your bill and make it eight hundred."

The master commended the dishonest manager because he had acted shrewdly.

Luke 16:1–8

It's not hard to see why people have responded to this passage with confusion. After all, it seems to condone dishonesty—not the kind of teachings we usually associate with Jesus.

Looking more closely, however, it's clear Jesus was not recommending negative behaviors. He explains the point immediately thereafter (vv. 8–9):

The people of this world are more shrewd in dealing with their own kind than are the people of the light. I tell you, use worldly wealth to gain friends for yourselves, so that when it is gone you will be welcomed into eternal dwellings.

This is a story about astuteness, not deception.

Jesus was advocating that believers observe how cleverly nonbelievers use their money in order to invest in and advance their agendas. He wanted His followers to use money as a tool to advance His agenda in the world.

In other words, He wanted His followers to invest worldly resources in order to produce a spiritual return.

Believe it or not, we need to understand that principle in order to understand Bilbo Baggins's actions in chapter 15 of *The Hobbit*.

A Sound Investment

This chapter's main action centers on Bilbo's surprisingly covert operation into the combined camp of the elves and men. Before getting there, however, we need to explore the motivation for his mission.

Things get started when Roäc returns and informs Thorin that his cousin Dain and more than five hundred dwarves from the Iron Hills are two days from the Lonely Mountain. Thorin is happy about the news, because he feels that reinforcements will force the hands of Bard and Thranduil the elf. Bilbo is not happy about the news, as it means he probably will remain a long time under the mountain with nothing to eat but elven bread.

Side note: Roäc once again gives Thorin wise advice, this time much more bluntly. He reminds Thorin that even five hundred grim allies are not enough to break the siege; even if they were, everyone still would be without food and supplies for the winter. He declares that the gold will be the king's death—even with Smaug out of the picture.

Thorin doesn't listen. Still wallowing in the deep folly of his corruption and greed, he refuses to consider the possibility that he's acting foolishly.

A BIG DECISION

Having witnessed this conversation, Bilbo sees what is about to happen. Either a battle will break with dwarves on one side, elves and men on the other, or the two armies will remain at a stalemate through the winter, lacking food and supplies. Either way, the result is bitterness, bloodshed, and death.

In that moment, he makes a big decision—one that will affect everyone in and around the mountain. And he wastes no time carrying it out: Later that night, he leaves the fortress within the Lonely Mountain and makes his way into the camp of the elves and men.

There he tells Bard and Thranduil about the dwarves being only two days' march from their camp. More, he presents Bard with the Arkenstone and encourages him to use it as leverage for striking a bargain with Thorin.

These are bold moves—staggering moves, really, considering all that we've seen from the hobbit throughout the story. Bilbo's actions reveal facets of his character we haven't seen before.

And so we're presented with serious questions: Is Bilbo acting wisely or foolishly? Is this a good development or something more sinister? Can we be proud of his actions, or should we be worried—even ashamed?

In light of what's happened since Thorin and the dwarves took hold of the treasure, we have to wonder whether Bilbo has become addled by riches as well. Even worse, do his acts signify a return to his "old self"? Is he betraying his friends to recapture his hobbit-hole comfort and security at any cost?

Fortunately, we don't have to wait long to answer these questions.

A Good Decision

Bard and Thranduil are stunned, understandably, when Bilbo presents them with the stone. The Elvenking recovers first and recommends that Bilbo remain with the elves in his camp. He knows dwarves, generally speaking, and is sure Thorin won't look upon the hobbit's actions with kindness.

Bilbo refuses. He doesn't want to abandon his friends after all they've been through together. Oh, and he promised to wake Bombur at midnight.

Just like that, we have our answers to the motives behind his actions.

He has not been addled or changed by his proximity to the treasure. Rather, he is grounded to the point where he worries about keeping his word to Bombur even amid everything that's happening around him.

Nor is Bilbo open to betraying his friends to escape the mountain and return to the soothing convenience of Bag End. Instead, he willingly returns to the cold, cheerless tunnels—to Thorin's grim mood and eating nothing but cram day after day. And he does so through the same simple goodness and depth of character that has served him so well through his adventures.

Any possible remaining doubts about his actions are erased by a sudden appearance from Gandalf while Bilbo is making his way from the camp. The wizard claps the hobbit on the back and repeats his words from back at the start: "There is always more about you than anyone expects!"[1]

Leadership Lessons From Bilbo Baggins

That raises another interesting question: If Bilbo's bold actions weren't a demonstration of cunning or betrayal, what were they? What new quality has he achieved that enabled him to form and execute such a daring plan?

The answer is leadership.

Recently we have seen Bard and Thranduil display

virtues associated with effective leadership. By contrast, we've also seen the examples of Thorin and the Master of Esgaroth. Now it's Bilbo's turn to teach us a few things.

TRUE LEADERS TAKE ACTION

Bilbo has demonstrated many honorable qualities—courage, wisdom, compassion, and common sense, to name a few. But one attribute we have not much seen from the hobbit is assertiveness. That changes now.

We know that Bilbo had been hanging on to the Arkenstone for several days, and that the beginnings of a plan had been forming in his mind. But when Roäc delivers the news of Dain's coming, Bilbo grasps what's about to happen and acts quickly. He doesn't hesitate or vacillate between decisions—he takes action that very night in order to make a play for peace.

We also see Bilbo's newfound assertiveness when he is confronted by the watchmen of the elves. The hobbit has always been fond of elves, and early on in his journey he treated them with a kind of reverence. But when the chips are down, he conveys in no uncertain terms that he must speak with Bard and the Elvenking and that they must take him to the center of the camp.

This mix of gentleness and boldness reflects the leadership of several biblical characters, including the apostle John. Through his letters, John regularly offered encouragement and wisdom to the different churches under his care. At times, however, he used sharper words to make a deeper impact.

This portion of his third epistle is a good example:

> I wrote to the church, but Diotrephes, who loves to be first, will not welcome us. So when I come, I will call attention to what he is doing, spreading malicious nonsense about us.
>
> 3 John 9–10

Equally impressive is that Bilbo acted even though it wasn't necessary for him to do so. It would have been tempting to leave the weightier matters in the hands of "experts"—Thorin and Bard and the other leaders of their people.

By doing what he knew was right, Bilbo avoided any sins of omission:

> If anyone, then, knows the good they ought to do and doesn't do it, it is sin for them.
>
> James 4:17

True Leaders Have a Moral Compass

Make no mistake about it: these decisions Bilbo makes carry with them a great deal of risk. Had he erred in his judgment, the consequences could have been disastrous for elves, men, dwarves—and especially himself.

The reason Bilbo is able to make a solid plan of action—and then stay firm in his decision—is that he possesses a reliable moral compass. He knows the difference between right and wrong.

This ability to choose right is an essential component of leadership.

When Solomon was about to ascend to Israel's throne, God appeared in a dream and said: "Ask for whatever you want me to give you" (1 Kings 3:5).

Here's what Solomon asked for:

> Now, Lord my God, you have made your servant king in place of my father David. But I am only a little child and do not know how to carry out my duties. Your servant is here among the people you have chosen, a great people, too numerous to count or number. So give your servant a discerning heart to govern your people and to distinguish

between right and wrong. For who is able to govern this great people of yours?

1 Kings 3:7–9

Solomon asked for the ability to discern so that he could make the tough choices as a leader. We often refer to this ability as wisdom, but it all starts with possessing a moral compass—knowing the difference between right and wrong, and having the strength of character to choose what's right.

Unfortunately for Solomon (and the people of Israel), he lost his moral compass after many years as king. He built a harem and filled it with literally hundreds of wives. He acquired thousands of horses and accumulated great piles of wealth. All of these were in direct disobedience to what, in Deuteronomy, God had commanded of His kings.

Fortunately for Bilbo (and the other inhabitants of Middle-earth), his compass never wavers. Even after all his life-threatening and life-changing adventures, Bilbo retains his wise and compassionate understanding of right and wrong. He gains even more of the character strength necessary to choose right over wrong—and it serves him very well.

The Golden Scale

Speaking of wisdom, take a moment to consider these words of Jesus:

> Do not store up for yourselves treasures on earth, where moths and vermin destroy, and where thieves break in and steal. But store up for yourselves treasures in heaven, where moths and vermin do not destroy, and where thieves do

not break in and steal. For where your treasure is, there
your heart will be also.

Matthew 6:19–21

"Treasure" is a dominant force in *The Hobbit*'s final
chapters. Smaug's hoard is the biggest motivating factor behind the maneuvers and machinations taking place between
people groups—dwarves, elves, men, and even goblins.

In recent chapters we've seen the dwarves be measured
on the "golden scale" of Smaug's treasure—and found
wanting. Their lust for wealth led them down a path of
foolishness, cruelty, and poor choices. In the next chapter
we'll see Bard and Thranduil take their turns on that scale.
They won't fare as well as we'd expect, given their past
demonstrations of wisdom and compassion.

It almost seems we should reconfigure Jesus' words:
"Do not store up for yourselves treasures in Middle-earth,
where dwarves hoard, where men and elves make war, and
where dragons break in and plunder."

In all the hubbub surrounding the tremendous fortune
within the bowels of the Lonely Mountain, it's easy to
overlook Bilbo's willingness to surrender the Arkenstone.
But that would be a mistake. In the face of entire armies
fighting and scrabbling and clawing to clutch the treasure, Bilbo's readiness to give it away is one of the more
significant events in the entire story.

Make no mistake: Bilbo wants the Arkenstone; he's
loath to give it up. The gem captivated him the moment
he first set eyes on it; he wants to keep it so badly that he's
risked Thorin's wrath by hiding it away for several days.

But what makes Bilbo so special is that, even more than
he desires the stone, he desires peace. He's willing to let go
of one of the world's most magnificent treasures so that
lives will be spared and relationships mended.

Remember also that the Arkenstone represents his entire share. Think about it: All the miles traveled, all the meals missed, all the danger overcome have been compressed into one glittering jewel. And Bilbo gives it away.

Truly, the hobbit is storing up treasures not on earth but in heaven. Truly, his heart is in the right place.

> No one can serve two masters. Either you will hate the one and love the other, or you will be devoted to the one and despise the other. You cannot serve both God and money.
>
> Matthew 6:24

Several times Bilbo has proven himself an Agent of Providence—a representative of Ilúvatar, the divine Creator. And he proves it again by giving away the Arkenstone and demonstrating that the treasure is not his master.

Indeed, the characters least interested in the treasure—Gandalf, Bilbo, the eagles—are Agents of Providence. They all serve God instead of money.

Literary Corner: The Arkenstone

Before moving to the Battle of Five Armies, I need to highlight another example of Tolkien's proficiency with foreshadowing. Bilbo's willingness to give up the Arkenstone for the greater good foreshadows one of the most important moments of his future.

> Bilbo took the envelope, but just as he was about to set it by the clock, his hand jerked back, and the packet fell on the floor. Before he could pick it up, the wizard stooped and seized it and set it in its place. A spasm of anger passed swiftly over the hobbit's face again. Suddenly it gave way to a look of relief and a laugh.
>
> "Well, that's that," he said. "Now I'm off!"[2]

If you've read *The Lord of the Rings*, you know "the envelope" contained the One Ring. In all the history of Middle-earth, Bilbo is one of only two beings to ever willingly surrender the One Ring. (The other is Samwise Gamgee, who returned the ring to Frodo after bearing it for a brief time.)

Just like Bilbo's present ability to give up the Arkenstone saved numerous lives, his future ability to walk away from the power of the Ruling Ring would pave the way for a bright future within Middle-earth.

We can't say for sure whether the two incidents are related. We can't be certain that willingness to relinquish the Arkenstone eventually helped Bilbo let go of the most powerful object in the world. But it certainly didn't hurt.

In either case, both instances prove that Bilbo Baggins's strength of character far exceeds his physical stature.

17

The War With Two Sides

rawing from Tolkien's major stories—*The Hobbit*, *The Lord of the Rings*, *The Silmarillion*—there are more than twenty types of sentient beings to be found within the borders of Middle-earth.

Some recently have become commonplace, such as elves, dwarves, trolls, dragons. Others are more exotic—ents, river-maids, barrow-wights, wargs. And it's a testament to Tolkien's imagination that a few of his creations are so fantastical that even yet they stand alone within a crowded genre. Who but Tolkien could conceive of the Nazgúl? Who else could write about Balrogs?

In spite of this incredible diversity, all of Tolkien's creations can be compartmentalized into two main categories: good and evil.

A number of whole species fit into those camps. There are no good goblins, for instance, nor are there any evil elves. Most people groups are divided, with individuals choosing to take a place within the forces of good (e.g., Aragorn) or of evil (e.g., the Ringwraiths).

In chapter 17 of *The Hobbit*, ten different groups participate in the Battle of Five Armies. Only three—goblins, wolves, and wargs—represent the forces of evil. The rest make up an impressively diverse coalition of good: elves, men, dwarves, eagles, a wizard, a skin-changer (Beorn), and a hobbit.

Sadly, their unity during the Battle of Five Armies only serves to highlight the tragedy of what almost happened before the battle even started.

Division and Discord

Up to now, *The Hobbit* has been a relatively whimsical tale. The characters have experienced hard times and even life-threatening danger. Still, through it all, the adventure's tone and tenor has remained positive, even humorous.

There's nothing humorous about the beginning of chapter 17. It's the low point of the story on a variety of levels.

For starters, when Thorin learns about the Arkenstone, his behavior toward Bilbo is contemptible. He shakes the hobbit like a rabbit, curses him, and calls him a descendant of rats. Then he picks up his onetime friend and companion—who has twice saved his life and the lives of his people—and would have dashed him on the rocks below if not for Gandalf's intervention.

In the end, Thorin sends Bilbo away with no payment for his services but vindictive and abusive words. It's the lowest moment in his brief career as King under the Mountain, and even the other dwarves are ashamed of him.

It's not the lowest moment of the chapter, however. That comes when the forces of good turn against each other out of desire for gold and jewels.

The dwarves are on one side, led by Thorin and Dain. We don't learn much about Dain throughout the story, but we're told that he and his people "burned"[1] with the knowledge that the Arkenstone was in Bard's hands. So it's reasonable to assume that they were affected by the same lust for gold that had consumed Thorin and the other dwarves inside the mountain.

On the conflict's other side, the armies of men and elves are led by Bard and Thranduil. Those two thus far have demonstrated wisdom through their actions, but now they take a step back. Bard seems almost eager for a fight when Dain and his five hundred companions come within view, noting that his forces would gain easy victory because of their high position on the spurs.

Thranduil's counsel seems wiser—at first glance. He says he's willing to wait a while longer before he begins a war for gold. But he also makes it clear that the dwarves cannot pass into the mountain without their leave and that the combined forces of Bard's men and the elves are enough to win a battle if they must.

In reality, Bard and Thranduil are of the same mind. Both leaders believe they possess a military advantage; both are willing to destroy the dwarves in order to maintain their siege of the mountain—and to keep their claim on the treasure.

By taking such a stance, both turn their backs on Bilbo's gift the night before. For peace, the hobbit relinquished his claim; both Bard and Thranduil praised him for it. But when they have opportunity to do the same—to let go of the gold to preserve peace and avoid bloodshed—both refuse. When Dain's dwarves charge forward to attack,

the armies of elves and men (and their leaders) are ready
to respond violently to claim what they've been promised.

These events bring to mind several biblical passages,
most notably Jesus' admonition that "Any kingdom divided against itself will be ruined, and a house divided
against itself will fall" (Luke 11:17), and Hebrews 13:5:
"Keep your lives free from the love of money and be content
with what you have, because God has said, 'Never will I
leave you; never will I forsake you.'"

The main underlying theme is that evil benefits when
the forces of good become divided. That's what the apostle
Paul was so desperate for the young church in Corinth to
understand:

> I appeal to you, brothers and sisters, in the name of our
> Lord Jesus Christ, that all of you agree with one another
> in what you say and that there be no divisions among you,
> but that you be perfectly united in mind and thought. My
> brothers and sisters, some from Chloe's household have
> informed me that there are quarrels among you. What I
> mean is this: One of you says, "I follow Paul"; another, "I
> follow Apollos"; another, "I follow Cephas"; still another,
> "I follow Christ."
>
> 1 Corinthians 1:10–12

The X-factor in the conflict over the treasure is that the
dwarves are clearly in the wrong. Thorin has made dreadful
choices since Smaug was destroyed; Dain's arrival spurs
him even to break his promise to relinquish Bilbo's share
of the treasure in exchange for the Arkenstone. More,
Dain and his dwarves are the aggressors—they attack the
armies of elves and men.

Even so, the decision to match their aggression is inexcusable. Choosing to fight, Bard and Thranduil risk
a serious rift within the forces of good. More, they risk

their own moral character by prioritizing treasure over peace.

Again, these are exactly Paul's concerns for his friends in Corinth. Paul knew that divisions among them would only cause damage—corporately and individually—and would limit the church's effectiveness as a force for good:

> The very fact that you have lawsuits among you means you have been completely defeated already. Why not rather be wronged? Why not rather be cheated? Instead, you yourselves cheat and do wrong, and you do this to your brothers and sisters.
>
> 1 Corinthians 6:7–8

He also knew, and tried to help them understand, that their squabbles were foolish because of everything they'd already been given through Jesus:

> So then, no more boasting about human leaders! All things are yours, whether Paul or Apollos or Cephas or the world or life or death or the present or the future—all are yours, and you are of Christ, and Christ is of God.
>
> 1 Corinthians 3:21–23

For dwarves and elves and men, to squabble over gold is as foolish. *Both* the winners and losers of a battle would have been destroyed by the hordes of goblins swarming toward the mountain—and all the treasure taken far away.

Divine Authority

Fortunately for the dwarves and elves and men—and a certain hobbit—their bickering and posturing didn't result in violence. But that has little to do with their wisdom or self-control and everything to do with divine intervention.

As a devout Catholic, Tolkien had a high view of God's sovereignty. He believed that everything and everyone ultimately served God's divine will. That included people who intentionally obey His will, people who are in rebellion against Him, even the forces of evil at work within the world.

These convictions are reflected strongly in the progression and outcome of the Battle of Five Armies.

THE FORCES OF EVIL

Isn't it interesting that the forces of evil arrived at the Lonely Mountain just in time to prevent the forces of good from killing each other? If the goblins had delayed their assault even a few hours—certainly if they'd waited for nightfall and the cover of darkness—they would have found an enemy already half-defeated and the treasure theirs for the taking.

But the goblins don't delay. In their greed and lust for blood, they hasten on for several nights and come into the open at the perfect moment to save the day for the armies of dwarves and elves and men—and for a certain hobbit.

Tolkien makes a fascinating statement through these events: Even the forces of evil serve the will of Providence. Even these can become Agents of Providence in order to accomplish the Creator's good purposes.

And this is a thoroughly biblical concept.

Look at the life of Joseph, for example. At age seventeen, his brothers beat him and sold him as a slave due to raging jealousy that their father loved him best. Their actions were wholly evil. They intended harm, and only harm.

And yet God achieved an abundance of good through those actions. After thirteen years of suffering, Joseph became the second-most powerful man in all of Egypt. During a seven-year famine, his wise counsel saved the lives of thousands—including those of his brothers.

When they eventually confessed and begged forgiveness, Joseph made it clear: God was at work throughout the entire situation to accomplish His will.

> You intended to harm me, but God intended it for good to accomplish what is now being done, the saving of many lives.
>
> Genesis 50:20

As we've seen, Paul affirmed this view of divine sovereignty:

> We know that in all things God works for the good of those who love him, who have been called according to his purpose.
>
> Romans 8:28

In the same way that all things—intentionally or unintentionally—submit to God's will in this world, Tolkien built Middle-earth so that even the vilest of creatures ultimately become the Creator's servants.

THE REBELLIOUS KING

Not only do the evil creatures serve the will of Ilúvatar, but so also do those who rebel against their call to be the Creator's servants.

We've seen that Thorin Oakenshield is tragically flawed. As a king, he's to represent the Creator among his people; he's to rule with wisdom and compassion, courage and grace. But in the end, Thorin does not fulfill his calling. He succumbs to the corruptions of greed and leads his people astray.

Yet in the hands of his Creator, he is not wholly lost. Even one such as Thorin can be used by Providence to accomplish good.

We see it when Thorin and the other dwarves burst from the mountain in the middle of the battle. As the dwarves charge into battle, they're clothed in shining armor, and a red light leaps from their eyes. Thorin himself gleams "like gold in a dying fire."[2]

This, Thorin's last act as leader of his people, is his finest hour. He runs fearlessly into the fray, wielding his axe with deadly force. When he calls for elves, men, and dwarves to join the attack, his voice booms like a horn in the valley. Those who hear, obey—for finally he *is* King under the Mountain.

Pressed into the service of the Creator, we finally see Thorin as he was meant to be. We see his potential realized. In that moment, the power and nobility of what he could have been—*should* have been—only heightens the sad reality of his rebellion, his corruption, and his coming death.

In this way, Thorin's story reflects that of Samson.

Made to be both ruler and warrior, Samson was blessed with supernatural strength and the opportunity to rescue Israel from Philistine oppression. But he squandered his gifts and eventually fell into disobedience and corruption.

Yet like Thorin, he was not wholly lost. In his last moments, Samson was given the chance to once again serve his Creator—to become, even briefly, the man he was created to be. And, like Thorin, he took advantage:

> Now the rulers of the Philistines assembled to offer a great sacrifice to Dagon their god and to celebrate, saying, "Our god has delivered Samson, our enemy, into our hands. . . ."
> When they stood him among the pillars, Samson said to the servant who held his hand, "Put me where I can feel the pillars that support the temple, so that I may lean

against them." Now the temple was crowded with men and women; all the rulers of the Philistines were there, and on the roof were about three thousand men and women watching Samson perform. Then Samson prayed to the Lord, "Sovereign Lord, remember me. Please, God, strengthen me just once more, and let me with one blow get revenge on the Philistines for my two eyes." Then Samson reached toward the two central pillars on which the temple stood. Bracing himself against them, his right hand on the one and his left hand on the other, Samson said, "Let me die with the Philistines!" Then he pushed with all his might, and down came the temple on the rulers and all the people in it. Thus he killed many more when he died than while he lived.

Judges 16:23, 25–30

The Agents of Providence

Of course, it's not only the rebellious and the forces of evil who are used to accomplish the Creator's will. Those who have been serving Providence throughout the story continue to do so during the Battle of Five Armies.

It's Gandalf, for example, who steps between the charging dwarves and the besieging army in order to announce the arrival of the goblins. And it's Gandalf who gathers the leaders from dwarves, elves, and men in order to draw up plans for attack and defense.

But it's the eagles—the heralds of Manwë sent to watch over the northern mountains—who do the heavy lifting in terms of actually turning the tide. When all hope seems lost and even Bilbo despairs, the eagles arrive as sharp-eyed, sharp-taloned manifestations of *deus ex machina*. Serving as Agents of Divine Rescue and Wrath, they toss the shrieking goblins from the mountainside and save the day for the forces of good.

Beorn plays a similar role. He charges through the mass to rescue Thorin, then back in again to rout the bodyguard of Bolg and crush the goblin-king once and for all. Even little Bilbo gets in on the act—it's he who first spots the eagles and sends news of their rescue echoing down the valley.

Necessary Violence

If *The Hobbit*'s seventeenth chapter differs from the rest of the book in overall tone, it also represents a change in depiction of violence and violent detail.

The earlier portions do contain violent moments, but these are diffused by lighthearted narration. For example, when trolls capture the dwarves, they speak of roasting or boiling them or squashing them all down to jelly. But the incident is played off as a joke, and amid the humor we're never convinced anything truly bad will happen.

When they emerge from their barrels after escaping the Elvenking in Mirkwood, Dori, Nori, Ori, Oin, and Gloin are described as "waterlogged" and "only half alive."[3] But those statements are offset by Fili complaining that his barrel smelled so strongly of apples, he hopes never again to see one.

Not so now. The Battle of Five Armies is thoroughly solemn and serious—even reminiscent of the battle scenes from *The Lord of the Rings*.

A charge of elves leaves the rocks "stained black with goblin blood,"[4] and wolves go about "rending the dead and wounded,"[5] and then goblins were stacked in heaps "till Dale was dark and hideous with their corpses."[6] There are slain members of the forces of good—men, dwarves, and "many a fair elf."[7] And in chapter 18, Bilbo converses with the mortally wounded Thorin, who is dying after being "pierced with spears."[8]

The contrast with the rest of the book is so sharp that we really are forced to ask why. Why would Tolkien include such violence in what many have considered a children's book?

The first of multiple answers is that Tolkien's descriptions once again reflect Scripture. Many wars and many battle scenes detailed in the Old Testament are visceral to the point of gruesome.

This account is one example:

> Amaziah then marshaled his strength and led his army to the Valley of Salt, where he killed ten thousand men of Seir. The army of Judah also captured ten thousand men alive, took them to the top of a cliff and threw them down so that all were dashed to pieces.
>
> Meanwhile the troops that Amaziah had sent back and had not allowed to take part in the war raided towns belonging to Judah from Samaria to Beth Horon. They killed three thousand people and carried off great quantities of plunder.
>
> 2 Chronicles 25:11–13

Second, Tolkien thought of himself as a sub-creator when writing even these scenes. He was engaged in creating a Secondary World sufficiently believable to help his readers become fully immersed in the story. And given what he went through, likely he could find nothing believable about a blithe or lighthearted conflict between multiple armies. He could find the humor in a confrontation with bumbling trolls, but nothing was humorous about war.

In *Tolkien and the Great War*, John Garth explains how battlefield experiences influenced "The Fall of Gondolin," Tolkien's first step on the narrative journey leading to *The Hobbit* and *The Lord of the Rings*:

The vivid extremes of the Somme, its terrors and sorrows, its heroism and high hopes, its abomination and ruin, seem to have thrown his vision of things into mountainous relief. A bright light illuminated the world and raised awful shadows. In this tale, Tolkien's mythology becomes, for the first time, what it would remain: a mythology of the conflict between good and evil.[9]

Third, he wrote seriously about the Battle of Five Armies because he had a serious view of spiritual warfare. In his mind, the supernatural clash between good and evil was as real as anything he endured during physical battle in the Great War. Thus, this metaphysical conflict had a similar impact on his work.

Tolkien understood that the devil "prowls around like a roaring lion looking for someone to devour" (1 Peter 5:8); therefore, the evil characters within his stories are fearsome and able to cause massive harm. He knew also that "our struggle is not against flesh and blood, but against the rulers, against the authorities, against the powers of this dark world and against the spiritual forces of evil in the heavenly realms" (Ephesians 6:12)—and so he was ruthless in destroying the forces of evil within his Secondary World.

18

Beyond the Veil

What comes to mind when you see the phrase "happily ever after"? These words at the end of many stories we call fairy tales elicit different reactions from different people. Some find this a charming way to end a story; others find it enjoyable in a childish sort of way; others think it cheesy, in poor taste.

Tolkien leaned very much toward the "charming" perspective. He held that a happy ending was vital to the success of any fairy story. Fortunately, his ideals for such an ending left no room for anything tacky or trite.

He was so adamant about the value of a specific happy-ending type that to describe it he invented a word: *eucatastrophe*, a word he defines here, taken from the essay "On Fairy-Stories" (referenced in Part 1) as:

the good catastrophe, the sudden joyous "turn" . . .[1]

Tolkien believed the best stories contain a moment that catches readers off guard and allows them to be impacted, moved, even changed through the story's power.

In *The Hobbit*, the eucatastrophe begins at the end of chapter 17 when Bilbo cries out, "The Eagles! The Eagles! The Eagles are coming!"[2] The "sudden turn" continues through the beginning of chapter 18, where we learn more details about the eagles' attack on the goblins and Beorn's unforeseen arrival and massive contribution to the goblins' defeat.

Yet even those happy moments are balanced by a touch of sadness—a poignant moment that does indeed carry the potential to inspire tears.

A Parting

The Bible has a lot to say about death. More, it has a lot to say about specific people who died—even providing a narrative glimpse into the final moments of several individuals.

For example, after a long and fulfilling life, "Then Abraham breathed his last and died at a good old age, an old man and full of years; and he was gathered to his people" (Genesis 25:8).

Stephen, one of the leaders of the early church, departed this life in a way that was far less peaceful but ultimately glorious:

> While they were stoning him, Stephen prayed, "Lord Jesus, receive my spirit." Then he fell on his knees and cried out, "Lord, do not hold this sin against them." When he had said this, he fell asleep.
>
> Acts 7:59–60

Not surprisingly, death plays an important role in Tolkien's mythology. Certain characters wrestle with it in all his major works. Many are grievously wounded, and while some recover or are rescued, others perish.

In *The Hobbit*, Thorin Oakenshield and Fili and Kili experience death's sting.

While Fili and Kili perish in defense of their king during the heat of the battle, Thorin survives to the following morning. This enables him to have a final—and poignant—conversation with Bilbo.

We learn early in chapter 18 that Thorin has specifically summoned Bilbo. More, when the hobbit arrives at the tent, Thorin greets him with the words, "Farewell, good thief."[3] Given what happened with the Arkenstone, not to mention their last encounter, these are unexpected words indeed.

So we wonder what's changed his attitude so quickly and completely.

GODLY SORROW

But we don't have to wonder long. After explaining that he is about to die, Thorin makes two indelibly encouraging statements to Bilbo.

First, the dwarf notes that he's leaving behind all gold and silver in order to go where such things are of little worth. His words are a direct parallel to the words of Jesus in Matthew 6:19–20:

Do not store up for yourselves treasures on earth, where moths and vermin destroy, and where thieves break in and steal. But store up for yourselves treasures in heaven, where moths and vermin do not destroy, and where thieves do not break in and steal.

We feel great relief when Thorin speaks these words that confirm his madness has ended. The prospect of imminent death has freed him from lust for wealth and gives him leave to finish out his last moments in relative peace.

Thorin's second statement is that he seeks a renewed friendship with Bilbo. The king offers to take back his earlier maltreatment of the hobbit—he repents of his recent deeds. He admits he was wrong and asks Bilbo's forgiveness.

Repentance is a primary biblical theme and a major part of spiritual growth for Christians. Those who follow Christ must first admit the error and futility of their old way of life—they must turn away from past attitudes and behaviors to accept God's offer of salvation and friendship.

Solomon learned the value of repentance from God himself:

> If my people, who are called by my name, will humble themselves and pray and seek my face and turn from their wicked ways, then I will hear from heaven, and I will forgive their sin and will heal their land.
>
> 2 Chronicles 7:14

The New Testament writers repeatedly emphasized repentance to the early church. For example, Paul rejoiced that his stern words had produced repentance among the believers in Corinth:

> I am happy, not because you were made sorry, but because your sorrow led you to repentance. For you became sorrowful as God intended and so were not harmed in any way by us. Godly sorrow brings repentance that leads to salvation and leaves no regret, but worldly sorrow brings death.
>
> 2 Corinthians 7:9–10

All this is important because it speaks to Thorin's chance to "finish well" despite pitfalls throughout his journey. We've watched him make a number of wrong turns lately—poor decisions, unquestionably, and foolish priorities, demonstrably—with disastrous consequences both for him and his people.

But it's a joyful thing that Thorin regains himself before his story ends. He turns away from those choices—he repents—and in doing so, he finds peace when it matters most. Further, he is able to speak openly, even eagerly, about joining his fathers in the "halls of waiting,"[4] and about the world being renewed. He has made peace with his Creator.

GODLY FORGIVENESS

There's an intriguing exchange at the beginning of chapter 18. It's quick, but it shows why Bilbo is such a good, wise, humble, and likeable character.

Bilbo had been knocked unconscious just before the eagles' arrival, and he remained that way overnight. When he wakes in the morning, he is alone and uncertain of the battle's outcome until he notices a few dwarves working at the gate of the mountain. Bilbo calls out when he sees a man approaching; the man obviously can't see the hobbit because of the ring. He asks, "What voice is it that speaks among the stones?"

The answer astonishes: "It's me, Bilbo Baggins, companion of Thorin."[5]

Companion of Thorin? Only two days before, the King under the Mountain had been cruel to him and expelled him from the company—he'd even picked him up and threatened to murder him viciously.

And yet, already, in his heart, Bilbo has forgiven Thorin. More, he still speaks of Thorin as a friend. Remember, this is *before* Bilbo knows Thorin is still alive, let alone that the dwarf has repented of those deeds. In this way, the hobbit reflects these instructions from Paul:

> Let all bitterness and wrath and anger and clamor and slander be put away from you, along with all malice. Be kind to one another, tenderhearted, forgiving one another, as God in Christ forgave you.
>
> Ephesians 4:31–32 ESV

Tenderhearted is an excellent description for Bilbo Baggins. When Thorin passes, the hobbit goes off by himself and weeps until his eyes become red and his voice becomes hoarse. Bilbo's forgiveness is so complete that he deeply feels the pain and loss of Thorin's death. He mourns his friend.

Eternity in Middle-Earth

Ecclesiastes 3:11 states that God "has put eternity into man's heart" (ESV). Tolkien agreed with this sentiment—although if he had included those words in some text within Middle-earth, he likely would have added, "and a dwarf's heart, and an elf's heart," and so on.

One of the more startling aspects of death's role in Tolkien's mythology is that death is never viewed as the end. Rather, the citizens of Middle-earth possess an understanding—even an expectation—of eternity.

Some people groups within this world—specifically elves, dwarves, and men—have a more defined understanding of what happens after death. So let's spend a few moments exploring the eschatology of Middle-earth.

ETERNITY FOR THE ELVES

We know more about life after death for the elves than any other inhabitants of Middle-earth—which is a bit ironic, since elves are immortal.

In Tolkien's realm, elves are connected to the world at a deep and powerful level. Like the Valar and Maiar, they endure as long as the world endures, and their spirits cannot depart from the world until it is broken and made new at the end of days.

Elves can be killed, though, which occurs several times in his major stories—including chapter 17 of *The Hobbit*. More accurately, their bodies can be cut down and separated from their spirits (or souls). When that happens, their spirits return to Valinor and dwell in the halls of Mandos. (Mandos, one of the Valar, is keeper of the halls of the dead.)

Elves whose spirits arrive in the halls of Mandos remain there for a long time in a kind of purgatory, contemplating their lives and awaiting the world to be remade (another connection with Tolkien's Catholicism). Some later notes compiled by Christopher Tolkien—most notably a book called *Morgoth's Ring*—suggest that elves can regain their bodies after a period of waiting, but that is not spelled out specifically in any major Tolkien work.

Eternity for the Dwarves

The dwarves of Tolkien's world are not immortal—they grow old and die as part of their nature, although they do live longer than men.

None of Tolkien's main stories includes a definitive plan for their life after death—if they do experience an afterlife. Indeed, according to *The Silmarillion*, many of the elves believe that dwarves return to the earth and stone from which they were made.

The dwarves themselves believe something quite different:

They say that Aulë the Maker, whom they call Mahal, cares for them, and gathers them to Mandos in halls set

apart; and that he declared to their Fathers of old that
Ilúvatar will hallow them and give them a place among
the Children in the End. Then their part shall be to serve
Aulë and to aid him in the remaking of Arda after the
Last Battle.[6]

In *The Hobbit*, Thorin confirms this belief when he
tells Bilbo, "I go now to the halls of waiting to sit beside
my fathers, until the world is renewed."[7]

ETERNITY FOR MEN

Human beings are different from elves and dwarves in
that their spirits (or souls) are unconnected from the world.
When men and women die, their spirits depart and go
somewhere else.

This departure is a mystery for the other inhabitants
of Middle-earth—not even the Valar know or understand
what happens to human souls after death. And for the
elves, who often weary of the world after thousands and
thousands of years, the fate of men sometimes seems like
a blessing.

Indeed, that's what Ilúvatar originally intended when
he created the "second born." For human beings, death
was a gift—a chance to escape weariness of the world
and move on to something new. More important, it's a
chance to join the Creator far sooner than elves and other
immortal beings.

In that way, Tolkien's world reflects our own.

The Bible reveals that humans were designed to be
immortal—we were created to spend eternity in fellowship with God. Because of our sin, the world around us
became a place of pain and doubt and death. More, we
also changed—we became enmeshed in sinful desires and
greed and violence.

God knew it would be torture for His children to live forever in a fallen, corrupted, pain-filled world. And so death offers us an escape—a chance to leave our broken bodies in a broken world and ultimately be reunited with God for eternity as He originally planned.

Viewed properly, then, death is a gift for us, just like it was a gift for the people of Tolkien's world. That's what allowed Paul to write things like this:

> To me, to live is Christ and to die is gain. If I am to go on living in the body, this will mean fruitful labor for me. Yet what shall I choose? I do not know! I am torn between the two: I desire to depart and be with Christ, which is better by far; but it is more necessary for you that I remain in the body.
>
> Philippians 1:21–24

Of course, plenty of people in our world see death as a curse rather than as a blessing. And the same is true within Tolkien's mythology.

For instance, the Númenórians were the mightiest and noblest race of men ever to set foot in Middle-earth. Because of their faithfulness to Ilúvatar and the Valar, they were blessed with exceptionally long lives—even up to five hundred years or more at their peak. As a result, the men of Númenor became wise, wealthy, and powerful.

Unfortunately, the more success and enjoyment they experienced in the physical world, the more hesitant they were to leave it. Over time, they became obsessed with death. Eventually they became terrified of it, and they sought any means to prevent or escape their parting from the world.

The Silmarillion records an illuminating confrontation between the men of Númenor and the heralds of the Valar. The Númenórians wanted to live in Valinor—the undying land—so they could possess eternal life like the elves. One of their arguments has to do with the necessity of faith, as they cannot be sure of what lies after death. Tolkien's brilliant technique here uses the Númenórians to highlight the two major obstacles that prevent men and women in our world from coming to peace with death's reality and looking forward to blessed eternity with God.

The first obstacle is that arriving at such a peace requires faith. Hebrews 11:1 proclaims that "faith is confidence in what we hope for and assurance about what we do not see." And that's the rub—even though we have been promised salvation and eternal life through God's Word, we have a hard time believing it without some kind of external evidence. We lack faith.

The second obstacle: *We also love the Earth and would not lose it.*

The Bible, especially the New Testament, shows notable separation between "the kingdom of God" and "the world." God's kingdom encompasses everything that works to accomplish His will. Everything else—all the temptations and desires and evil forces at work against His will—is referred to as "the world" or "the flesh." The two realms are mutually exclusive.

John highlighted this separation in one of his letters:

> Do not love the world or anything in the world. If anyone loves the world, love for the Father is not in them. For everything in the world—the lust of the flesh, the lust of the eyes, and the pride of life—comes not from the Father but from the world. The world and its desires pass away, but whoever does the will of God lives forever.
>
> 1 John 2:15–17

Many people say they have faith—that they believe in heaven and want to go there—but in the deep recesses of their hearts, they place a higher value on the world's comforts and pleasures. They don't want to leave.

That was a major obstacle for the Númenórians, and Tolkien brilliantly used that fictional culture to reveal our own misplaced values and priorities.

19

A New Creation

Perhaps I should have said so earlier, though you may already know: The full title of Tolkien's book is *The Hobbit, or There and Back Again*. Those five extra, seemingly superfluous words accurately describe the plot's movement.

As is the case with many journeys, especially the adventurous kind, the first half of Bilbo's story is much more interesting than the second—and so takes up the bulk of the telling. The first eighteen chapters focus on the "There" portion, and only now, in chapter 19, do we get some information about the "Back Again."

It's been a long road for Bilbo, and the overwhelming impression we get from him on the final leg of his tale is that he's weary and ready for the Shire. He wants to go home.

Now, this renewed desire for Bag End is not like those earlier moments when Bilbo pined over thoughts of his warm fire and fried eggs whenever he felt afraid or uncomfortable—it's not a longing for ease and security above everything else. Rather, he has accomplished his task, and he's ready for a time of rest after a job well done. He deserves it.

A Time to Sing

One of the final chapter's unique elements is the space taken up by songs. Its few pages contain three, complete with stanzas and choruses. Two belong to the elves; Bilbo writes the other, spontaneously, upon entering the Shire.

Actually, this is not a new facet. Looking over the whole book, we'll find several songs from several sources. These play two important roles within the story: establishing culture and memorializing key events.

Culture Songs

Almost all the different people groups represented in *The Hobbit* can be connected with some kind of song or prose. More important, the songs of each group are unique—they are distinctive from each other, and they reveal much about the cultures of those who sing them.

For example, each song of the elves communicates deep reverence and appreciation for the natural world. The elves in Rivendell sing about the loveliness of the valley they call home, and of the river that runs through its borders. The elves of Mirkwood sing about marshes and trees and stars while rowing toward Lake-town. And in chapter 19, the elves (again in Rivendell) sing about the beauty of fire and stars surpassing gold and silver.

The dwarves also sing several songs, although, not surprisingly, their verses are quite different from—even in direct contrast to—those of the elves'. At the unexpected party, for example, they sing about weaving the light of the sun and moon into precious jewels, and of catching light in the hilts of swords. That is, their songs also express what is most valuable within their culture.

There are also examples of prose in *The Hobbit*, like the riddles passed back and forth by Bilbo and Gollum in the roots of the Misty Mountains. These too reveal much about the worldview and experiences of the riddlers. Bilbo's riddles are quite cheerful and focus on things like eggs and flowers. Gollum's riddles, dark and menacing, speak of nothingness, corrosion, death.

Speaking of "menacing," even the goblins sing songs—and even they reveal their culture therein. After capturing Bilbo and the dwarves, they chant during their descent to the caves below: "Swish, smack! Whip, crack! Batter and beat! Yammer and bleat!"[1] (And that's just one of the verses.)

If we had to form an opinion on orcs based on songs (especially "Fifteen birds in five fir-trees," chapter 6), we'd easily discern their evil natures.

MEMORIAL SONGS

In addition to establishing culture, a few songs serve to memorialize important events. At the unexpected party once again, the dwarves sing about Smaug's attack on the Lonely Mountain and the destruction of Dale. In Laketown, the men sing about an event prophesied for the future—the return of the King under the Mountain and the river running full of gold.

These kinds of songs also are common in the Bible. Moses wrote a song after God miraculously saved Israel from the Egyptians at the sea (see Exodus 15). Deborah, a leader during the time of the judges, composed a similar song after her armies defeated the Canaanites in a major battle (see Judges 5).

In chapter 19, Bilbo, coming at last into view of his own hill and home, composes his own memorial song. He sings about the roads he's traveled, under trees and through caves and over grass and under mountains. He remembers the excitement and dread.

But Bilbo's song also flows from, and reveals, the values of his hobbit culture. We know this because the main idea behind his song is that all those roads lead back to the meadows and trees and hills he's known all his life.

Like him, the roads all return home.

A Tale of Two Hobbits

Just after this unplanned burst of song, Gandalf looks at his friend in wonder:

> "My dear Bilbo!" he said. "Something is the matter with you! You are not the hobbit that you were."[2]

This declaration is one of the book's most important moments. In fact, in many ways it represents the culmination of *The Hobbit*'s primary theme.

A NEW CREATION

Think back to the "party" at the start of Bilbo's adventure. He behaved pathetically that evening. He was rude. He bounced to and fro between terror and boastful pride. He was the antithesis of everything we expect in a hero.

Yet Gandalf saw something inside him that no one else could see—not even Bilbo. He knew Bilbo had been created for a special purpose, and he proclaimed with confidence that the hobbit would rise to the challenges if given the chance. More, he specifically and directly called Bilbo to join the adventure and become the hero he was created to be.

The dwarves were ready to give up on Bilbo after they escaped from the goblins and emerged on the other side of the mountains. The hobbit had been left behind (or so they thought), and they thought him more trouble than he was worth. Gandalf stood his ground and reaffirmed Bilbo's value. The wizard even went so far as to promise that, before the quest was over, the dwarves would thank him for recruiting Mr. Baggins.

He was right. Bilbo rose to the occasion. He grew in courage, advanced as a leader. In the forest of Mirkwood he exceeded every expectation, rescuing the dwarves from certain death, destroying a host of evil creatures. More, he conjured the plot to rescue them again from the prison of the Elvenking and so took his place as their leader.

At the Lonely Mountain he willingly confronted Smaug to serve his friends, twice. In doing so he won a decisive battle in his personal war against the fear and doubt that had plagued him all his life. He won a fight against greed by giving up his most treasured possession, seeking to secure peace.

Gandalf praised Bilbo for these actions, once again declaring, "There is always more about you than anyone expects!"[3] Even Thorin, on his deathbed, told the hobbit that he possessed more good than he knew.

Now, finally, Gandalf brings this theme full circle. No longer does he speak of Bilbo's untapped potential. No longer does he claim the hobbit has hidden virtues other people don't expect or are unable to see. Rather, as the quest ends, within sight of the Shire, Gandalf proclaims

Bilbo to be no longer the hobbit he was. He has become something new—something better.

At the end of Bilbo's story, he is a hero after all.

By emphasizing this theme throughout, Tolkien mirrors the process of spiritual growth for followers of Christ. Like Bilbo, we are products of a Creator, made and called to fulfill a specific purpose:

> Praise be to the God and Father of our Lord Jesus Christ, who has blessed us in the heavenly realms with every spiritual blessing in Christ. For he chose us in him before the creation of the world to be holy and blameless in his sight.
>
> Ephesians 1:3–4

Like Bilbo, we must grow in order to achieve that purpose. And like Bilbo, again, we usually grow best through trials and difficult circumstances:

> Consider it pure joy, my brothers and sisters, whenever you face trials of many kinds, because you know that the testing of your faith produces perseverance. Let perseverance finish its work so that you may be mature and complete, not lacking anything.
>
> James 1:2–4

Most important, when we respond to our Creator and work toward His purposes for our lives, we become something new—something better:

> If anyone is in Christ, the new creation has come: The old has gone, the new is here!
>
> 2 Corinthians 5:17

As a reminder, Tolkien was still acting as sub-creator when he wove this theme into *The Hobbit*. There isn't a direct connection between the points of Bilbo's journey and the stages of justification and sanctification. Rather, the hobbit's journey is a reflection of the transformation we experience through faith in Jesus. Bilbo's story is first and foremost a story, but it does help us see salvation and spiritual growth from a fresh angle.

Tolkien's writing here is brilliant—both entertaining and uplifting. Yet amazingly, it only takes a few paragraphs for him to do even better.

DEATH AND LIFE

When Bilbo finally arrives at his hobbit-hole—more than a year after departing without any pocket-handkerchiefs—he finds a large crowd trundling in and out, most of his furniture already carted away. Turns out he has been "Presumed Dead,"[4] and he arrives with Gandalf just in time to see the last of his possessions being auctioned off.

The amusing scene incorporates a number of light-hearted observations—especially regarding the Sackville-Bagginses. But we must not overlook the power and poignancy of what's taking place. Bilbo has been declared legally dead, and in many ways—the most important ways, at least—this is accurate.

The Bilbo Baggins we met at the beginning has in fact passed away. The Bilbo who was paralyzed by doubt and fear is no more. The hobbit who had no chance of surviving a perilous venture has indeed been killed by it—and someone new lives in his place.

Once again Tolkien uses Bilbo's situation as a reflection of our own experiences when it comes to the most vital aspects of the Primary World: salvation and transformation. Through Bilbo's "death," we are encouraged to take a creative look at what Paul describes:

If we have been united with him in a death like his, we will certainly also be united with him in a resurrection like his. For we know that our old self was crucified with him so that the body ruled by sin might be done away with, that we should no longer be slaves to sin—because anyone who has died has been set free from sin.

Romans 6:5–7

I mentioned in chapter 1 that Bilbo's adventure would be an opportunity to move away from his "old self" and become something new—become who he was created to be. Now Tolkien shows us that the hobbit's "old self" has been declared legally dead; Bilbo has been "made new."

As we reflect on the deeper themes at the foundation of Bilbo's story, we're reminded that we've been offered the same opportunity:

You were taught, with regard to your former way of life, to put off your old self, which is being corrupted by its deceitful desires; to be made new in the attitude of your minds; and to put on the new self, created to be like God in true righteousness and holiness.

Ephesians 4:22–24

As we put on our new selves, we may not be called to heroic exploits, but we will make an impact for the good, and that will have lasting implications into eternity.

These are vital truths for any world—Primary or Secondary, natural or supernatural—and they are the heart within the spiritual world of *The Hobbit*.

Notes

Introduction

1. J. R. R. Tolkien, *The Hobbit* (Boston: Houghton Mifflin, 1997), 245.

Part 1—Behind the Scenes

Chapter 1: Faërie and Fairy Stories

1. J. R. R. Tolkien, *Tales from the Perilous Realm* (Harper Collins, 2008), 315–316.
2. Ibid., 323.
3. Ibid., 327.
4. *The Letters of J. R. R. Tolkien*, Humphrey Carter, ed. (Boston: Houghton Mifflin, 2000), 288–289.

Chapter 2: Tolkien as Sub-Creator

1. Tolkien, *Tales from the Perilous Realm*, 363–364.
2. Collins English Dictionary—Complete & Unabridged 10th edition by HarperCollins. http://dictionary.reference.com/browse/allegory (accessed 01/31/12).
3. Tolkien, *Tales from the Perilous Realm*, 371.

Chapter 3: A Short History of Middle-Earth

1. J. R. R. Tolkien, *The Silmarillion* (New York: Del Ray/Random, 1999), 3.
2. Ibid., 4.
3. Ibid., 32

Part 2: Between the Pages

Chapter 1: A Comfortable Life

1. J. R. R. Tolkien, *The Hobbit* (Boston: Houghton Mifflin, 1997), back cover.
2. Ibid., 4.
3. Ibid., 15.
4. Ibid., 5.
5. Ibid., 19.

Chapter 2: A Poor Beginning

1. Tolkien, *The Hobbit*, 30.
2. Ibid., 32.
3. Tolkien, *The Hobbit*, 34.
4. Ibid., 38.
5. Tolkien, *The Silmarillion*, 360.
6. Ibid., 359–360.
7. See "The Window on the West" chapter in *The Two Towers*, Book II of *The Lord of the Rings*.

Chapter 3: An Old Friend

1. Tolkien, *The Hobbit*, 43.
2. Ibid., 48.
3. Tolkien, *The Silmarillion*, 194.
4. John Garth, *Tolkien and the Great War* (New York: HarperCollins, 2005), 216–218.

Chapter 4: Darkness and Light

1. Tolkien, *The Hobbit*, 56.
2. Tolkien, *The Silmarillion*, 6.

Chapter 5: Turning Points

1. Tolkien, *The Hobbit*, 64.
2. Ibid., 77.
3. Ibid., 78.
4. J. R. R. Tolkien, *The Fellowship of the Ring* (Boston: Houghton Mifflin, 1987), 69.

Chapter 6: Two Escapes

1. Tolkien, *The Hobbit*, 86.
2. Tolkien, *The Silmarillion*, 69.
3. Ibid., 65.
4. Ibid., 20.
5. Ibid., 18.

6. Tolkien, *The Silmarillion*, 16.
7. Ibid., 126.

Chapter 8: A New Hobbit

1. Tolkien, *The Hobbit*, 142.

Chapter 9: The Hidden Hero

1. Tolkien, *The Hobbit*, 161.
2. Ibid.
3. Ibid., 167.

Chapter 10: The Long-Awaited Party

1. J. Barton Payne, *Encyclopedia of Biblical Prophecy* (Grand Rapids: Baker, 1980).
2. James Stuart Bell, *The Bible Answer Book* (Sourcebooks, 2010), 82.
3. Tolkien, *The Silmarillion*, 38.
4. Tolkien, *The Hobbit*, 192.

Chapter 11: The Waiting Is the Hardest Part

1. Tolkien, *The Hobbit*, 182.
2. Ibid.
3. Ibid.
4. Carpenter, *Tolkien: A Biography*, 78.
5. Garth, *Tolkien and the Great War*, 104.
6. Tolkien, *The Hobbit*, 50.

Chapter 12: Bilbo's Two Battles

1. Tolkien, *The Hobbit*, 199.
2. J. R. R. Tolkien, from the lecture "Beowulf: The Monsters and the Critics," delivered 11/25/1936 (see at www.scribd.com).

Chapter 13: The Seeds of Greed

1. Tolkien, *The Hobbit*, 194.
2. Ibid.
3. Tolkien, *The Silmarillion*, 8.

Chapter 14: Whispers and Flame

1. Tolkien, *The Hobbit*, 221–222.
2. Ibid., 223.

Chapter 15: The King Under the Mountain

1. Ibid., 11.

Chapter 16: A Shrewd Hobbit

1. Tolkien, *The Hobbit*, 245.
2. Tolkien, *Fellowship of the Ring*, 43.

Chapter 17: The War With Two Sides

1. Tolkien, *The Hobbit,* 250
2. Ibid., 254.
3. Ibid., 175.
4. Ibid., 253.
5. Tolkien, *The Hobbit*, 254.
6. Ibid., 255.
7. Ibid.
8. Ibid., 260.
9. Garth, *Tolkien and the Great War*, 217.

Chapter 18: Beyond the Veil

1. Tolkien, *Tales from the Perilous Realm*, 384.
2. Tolkien, *The Hobbit*, 256.
3. Ibid., 258.
4. Ibid.
5. Tolkien, *The Hobbit*, 257.
6. Tolkien, *The Silmarillion*, 41.
7. Ibid., 258.

Chapter 19: A New Creation

1. Tolkien, *The Hobbit*, 58.
2. Ibid., 270.
3. Ibid., 245.
4. Ibid., 270.

James Stuart Bell is a Christian publishing veteran and the owner of Whitestone Communications, a literary development agency. He is the editor of many story collections including the CUP OF COMFORT and EXTRAORDINARY ANSWERS TO PRAYER series, and the coauthor of numerous books in THE COMPLETE IDIOT'S GUIDE series. He and his family live in West Chicago, Illinois.